Sun Lounges and Conservatories

CW00549437

Sun Lounges and Conservatories

JOCK DAVIDSON

W. Foulsham & Co. Ltd.

London · New York · Toronto · Cape Town · Sydney

W. Foulsham & Company Limited
Yeovil Road, Slough, Berkshire, SL1 4JH

ISBN 0–572–01312–4

Photoset in Great Britain by
Photobooks (Bristol) Ltd

Book design by Sally-Ann Grover
Illustrations by Michael Stringer

Thanks to Halls, Alexander Bartholomew,
Harry Smith Agency, E Saqui, P Blunden, R Aggiss,
E Slade, A Jacobs, Rochfords for help with the
photographs.

Printed in Spain by Cayfosa, Barcelona
Dep. leg. B - 6671-1985

*(Title page) When choosing a conservatory, make sure that it
complements the type of house. A Victorian structure would be
out of place on this modern house.* (Halls)

Contents

Conservatories come in all shapes and sizes. A small varnished wood conservatory used for growing tomatoes, begonias, gloxinias, cyclamen and geranium. (Taylor)

A larger, more elaborate varnished wood conservatory in a polygonal shape extends off the living room of this semi-detached house. (Bartholomew)

▲ A varnished wood conservatory which cleverly follows the slope of the house roof, complementing the house attractively. (Bartholomew)

▶ This stone sun lounge extends beside the garage and provides an extra room and a good environment for growing begonias. (P W Blunden)

An older style of conservatory, painted white to tie in with the house walls. (Bartholomew)

Conservatories do not have to be at ground level. Here the Victorian-style conservatory extends at first floor level. (Bartholomew)

Conservatories are usually positioned off the living room. Here the colourful display is viewed from the kitchen. (Smiths)

An aluminium framed conservatory avoids some of the problems of rot, warp and rust. (Halls)

Introduction

Today the term conservatory can be ascribed to almost any design of glass-covered area that one may attach to one's residence, but in the Victorian heyday of the conservatory such a building was essentially a home that was heated and used for accommodating exotic plants of one kind or another. In fact, in those days the building for housing plants might have been free-standing and some way from the main residence, but it was not in the accepted sense a greenhouse – greenhouses were used for the production of plants rather than their effective display.

Over the years conservatory design has become much less ornate with considerable emphasis on making maximum use of the interior of the structure once it has been erected. In Victorian days heating was provided by rows of cast-iron hot water pipes fitted to a solid-fuel boiler, whereas today heat can be supplied by a variety of means, with little or no clutter of pipes around the internal perimeter of the building. In some instances the design of the modern building amounts to little more than a conventional greenhouse that has been adapted to stand against the wall of the house – hence the term 'Lean-to'. Wherever possible, however, it is advisable to invest in a more solid structure.

Whereas the traditional conservatory is used purely for the purpose of displaying exotic plants, the modern equivalent may be referred to as a sun lounge that will become more of a leisure area than a plant area. In effect the sun lounge becomes an additional room, but such use should not preclude the use of plants for decoration and to offer an added feeling of relaxation. In this respect, modern office-type containers made from plastic or fibreglass are ideal for both growing plants and for setting them off to maximum effect.

The ornate metal work of the Victorian conservatory gave way to timber, and we now see the latter material being replaced to a great extent by lightweight aluminium. But this is not to say the elegant conservatories constructed mainly from wood are not available if one has the means to pay. At almost all modern garden exhibitions one will find a good selection of conservatories constructed from the various materials that are currently in use. The modern design of many of these conservatories will enhance the appearance and add much in the way of value to one's property.

Although not a conservatory in the conventional sense, the new 'range of glass' at Kew Gardens gives some indication of where we might be heading in respect of conservatory design. Massive girders set at low pitch are used to give the building an appearance of solidarity, and to ensure that the interior offers a clear expanse of space that is not unduly cluttered with upright roof supports. The cost of such a building is way beyond the means of the ordinary citizen, but such designs could well influence smaller edifices that may appear in the more humble back garden.

1Construction
& Maintenance

◀ *This timber-framed conservatory is an extension of the porch. Begonias and a variety of pelargoniums make the entrance colourful.* (P W Blunden)

▲ *Some manufacturers will design a conservatory to your requirements.* (Bartholomew)

Choosing a Conservatory

Surprising though it may seem, there are still tradesmen around who can build you a traditional Victorian conservatory if this is your wish. But let it be said that this would be a very costly addition to the homestead, and that when seeking a traditional conservatory it should be borne in mind that the house to which it is to be attached should be in keeping with the traditional structure.

Should the house be modern then it is preferable to invest in a building that will have modern lines that will blend more readily with the surroundings. Fine and solid though the Victorian conservatory may be, it will have its drawbacks in maintenance. The smaller sections of glass in the traditional building will mean that there is need for a great deal of woodwork in the way of glazing bars and such like to keep the glass in position. Also there is only one way to look after such buildings and that is to paint them white and to scrub down and re-paint the woodwork every second year. You should bear these drawbacks in mind when choosing your conservatory.

In many instances the conservatory is little more than a conventional greenhouse that has been adapted for the purpose, but when choosing, one should try to avoid very small structures as they become excessively hot and unpleasant. The covering material need not be glass and can be nothing more elaborate than corrugated plastic sheets that are clear to allow light through, or the budget may allow for newer materials such as polycarbonate sheets that are at present favoured by many commercial growers of plants.

The majority of modern conservatories come as complete units from the manufacturer who, at additional cost, will also take on the responsibility of erection. Or, if one wishes to take advantage of tax concessions there are manufacturers of conservatories who will supply their product in kit form for the new owner to put together – generally a simple operation if one follows the directions that are provided. Mention has been made elsewhere of the Feeder Greenhouse, the supply of which is generally offered at very competitive prices at Garden Centres and larger stores. These are simple to erect by the new owner, or can be erected by the supplier at additional cost.

When choosing a conservatory one should always opt for the largest possible size, presuming it is suited to both the site and one's pocket. The reason for selecting large as opposed to small is that no matter what area there is at the outset it will inevitably be too small as one's interest in plants develops. As mentioned elsewhere, one should also be selective when stocking the conservatory – the empty area may well appear daunting to begin with, but it is amazing how quickly the available space is filled once the bug for collecting plants begins to bite.

It is wise to discuss your planned conservatory with a local planning officer. Under the Town and Country Planning Act of 1971, conservatories do not need approval. A dwelling may be extended by up to $70 \, m^3$ more than its original size as long as the extension is to the side or the rear of the building.

Choosing a Site

Whether one is building a traditional conservatory or going along to the retailer's display area to select something that is appealing to the eye and a reasonable fit for the chosen site, it is important to do some preparatory work. More often than not, the siting of the conservatory is dictated by the arrangement of doors and windows around the house. The location that is normally chosen is directly outside the sitting room so that one can step through the french doors and into the green jungle or haven of peace. However, should there be a choice it is better to locate the conservatory on the east or west side of the building. If the conservatory is north facing it will tend to be very cold in winter and will be forever shaded from the sun by the building to which it is attached. On south facing walls there will be a continual battle to protect plants from the sun's rays, and to maintain cooler temperatures during the summer months, although the conservatory will be easier to manage and cost less during the winter. If the conservatory is free standing at some distance from the house in similar fashion to a greenhouse, then the best location is to have the ends of the building facing north-south. This sort of placement will ensure that plants benefit from the maximum amount of sunlight that is available.

When choosing your site think about what other uses your conservatory might have, apart from housing an exotic collection of plants. If you are going to use it as an extra room it needs to be large enough to accommodate furniture as well as plant displays, and if you are going to eat in it on sunny winter days you may find a site opening off the kitchen a convenient location.

Foundations – A Solid Base

Investment in a conservatory can be quite considerable, so it is as well to get things right at the outset, and this will certainly mean the provision of firm foundations. Regardless of the type of building that one intends to acquire, the first step must be to make a firm base on which it will stand. The inexperienced person would be well advised to contact one of the many local builders in the neighbourhood, perhaps more than one, in order that estimates for providing a solid base can be acquired.

While discussing requirements with the builder it will be wise to mention the need for him to make allowance for the installation of electricity, gas, water (a water point is almost essential) or whatever. Even if such things are never needed it will be a comfort to know that provision has been made and that one will not have to chisel out the concrete if a pipe of any kind has to be provided at a later date.

Also when the base is being laid the builder must make allowance for anchoring the building to prevent it taking off with the first gale of wind. The conservatory will obviously have to be firmly fixed to the main building, but it is also a wise precaution to ensure that the base is also securely anchored. A more attractive and more professional appearance will result if the base is fixed to a low brick wall rather than directly onto the concrete foundation.

An Adjacent Paved Area

If a patio area does not already exist adjacent to the conservatory site, it could well be wise to consider a paved area that can be laid as a natural extension to the conservatory while the foundations are being prepared. Such an area will prove to be invaluable as time goes on, and in particular when the conservatory is crowded with plants during the summer months and one is seeking additional space for them. Many of the conservatory plants can go out of doors from mid-May until late on in September. When brought indoors again they can be trimmed back, in particular fuchsias and geraniums, so that they occupy less space and will break fresh and more vigorously from new growth in the spring.

Many of the hanging plants can also be taken out of doors and given a sheltered location, although it may be necessary to bring them indoors at night during the first couple of weeks of May. On blustery or very cold days it will also be beneficial to take more vulnerable plants into the protection of the conservatory.

Building Your Own Conservatory From a Kit

Some conservatories, such as the aluminium-framed one illustrated overleaf, can be erected from a kit in a weekend. Once the base has been laid and obstructions such as drainpipes and manhole covers have been dealt with, preferably by a builder, you can begin to install the conservatory. In the example overleaf, the pre-drilled frame is first fixed to the wall of the house using a drill and the bolts provided. Then the frame is bolted together. Mastic is used to make a watertight seal between the metal ridge and the house wall. Pre-cut glass is then slotted into position and black capping is used to hold the glass in place. Finally the double sliding door is fitted.

Fixing the frame to the house wall. (Halls)

Bolting the frame together. (Halls)

Sealing with mastic to make a watertight seal between ridge and house wall. (Halls)

Installing pre-cut toughened glass curved sections. (Halls)

Fitting black capping to a glazing bar. (Halls)

Fitting the double sliding door. (Halls)

The completed conservatory built from a kit. (Halls)

Should You Have a Greenhouse as Well?

When the builder is on site dealing with the requirements for the conservatory it will not be a lot more
costly to get him to lay the foundations for the
greenhouse as well. Select the greenhouse, provide
the measurements and a walled base will appear
almost magically if the builder already has his
materials on hand.

As for the conservatory, the base should be
provided with bolts protruding from the brick base
with the intention that bolts will come through
appropriate holes in the base of the greenhouse so
that it can be securely fixed in position.

If one is to do the job thoroughly it will be
necessary to provide a water supply to the greenhouse, and the builder might well be able to put the
supply under the ground and connect everything up
for you. The ace handyman will, no doubt, be able to
undertake most of these jobs for himself, but the
builder is very useful when time and personal skills
are lacking, and the budget figure is not too critical.

It may well be felt that the greenhouse in itself is
a luxury, and quite extraneous to the exercise of
growing plants in a conservatory. The optimistic new
conservatory owner might feel that all the plants that
may be required to decorate the new addition to the
homestead can all be reared and cared for under one
roof. But years of experience in the field of growing
plants tells one that such thoughts are indeed very
optimistic, it being very much better to rear young
plants, pot them and such like in an area (such as the
nursery greenhouse) that is entirely divorced from
the conservatory.

2 Fitting Out the Conservatory

Choosing the Type of Flooring

The most important requirement once the concrete base has been laid will be to decide on the type of floor that one feels will be most suitable. Remember, when you are putting down the flooring that you may want to grow plants at floor level in the soil, so make sure you do not cover this area with slabs or tiling.

If you have a feeder greenhouse where all the dirty jobs can be done it would perhaps not be out of the way to consider carpeting the floor. Naturally, care would have to be taken when watering and suchlike, but if the conservatory is to serve the dual purpose of leisure area as well as plant sanctuary, then a carpet might well be the best choice. If all plants are then grown in watertight containers of the office landscaping type, one can create a pleasing blend of materials that can be rearranged with little difficulty.

For the dedicated plantsman, however, there is no question that the thought of carpeting the floor would be as welcome as toothache on a wet Sunday! For the plants and the plantsman who is to enjoy and care for them there is no doubt whatsoever that the 'feeling' of moistness that one can create in a glassed in area is of paramount importance – and there is no way that this sort of feeling can be achieved if a moisture-sapping carpet is laid on the floor. In the conservatory, even more so than in a conventional greenhouse, there is a continual battle for moisture – the plants are crying out for it, the flooring material (be it concrete or carpet) is crying out for it, and even the furniture and cushions if they are not plastic are crying out for and absorbing moisture.

Decorative ceramic tiles, provided they are not glossy and slippery, are probably the best bet for anyone wishing to have a pretty as opposed to functional conservatory. An important part of the care of the conservatory will be to retain a moist atmosphere, particularly during the summer months when plants dry out so alarmingly, so moisture must be introduced in every possible way. One of the most suitable ways of doing this is to keep the floor regularly damped over – several times each day during the summer. Only occasional damping in this way is needed in winter when there is always the

Wooden slat flooring

danger of getting plants too wet and creating a dank condition that will increase the incidence of fungal diseases. Because of the need to splash water around on the floor, you should consult the person responsible for the foundations with a view to providing a drain for surplus water, and perhaps a gentle slope in the floor towards the spot where the drain cover is located.

An alternative to a solid concrete base will be to provide a concrete surround on which the walls of the conservatory can be fixed and to lay paving slabs on a firm sand base within the conservatory. Like almost everything else, paving slabs have come a long way in recent years and you are not now restricted to simple squares of dull concrete under your feet. A visit to almost any good Garden Centre will give you an opportunity to inspect an extensive range of slabs in all shapes, colours and sizes, so there is no lack of choice. Where slabs are laid on sand there is no need for drainage as a rule because surplus water finds its way between the slabs to be dispersed in the sand. However, it is important that slabs are properly laid by someone with experience of the job, as heavy slabs on poor foundations can create all sorts of difficulties. One of the major benefits of having slabs on a sand base is the facility to lift and move them at any time should alterations to the original design be felt necessary.

Heating the Conservatory – Choosing a System

When deciding upon the form of heating to be installed you should make a thorough investigation at greenhouse retailing selling centres in your area, so that a comparison of the many designs on offer can be made. All have their individual merits, but some are bulky, some costly to install, some costly to run. It would, therefore, seem sensible to make a reasonable assessment of the various products on offer before any firm decisions are made.

▶ *Flooring: Paving slabs on a firm sand base make attractive flooring material for this traditional conservatory.*

Two different types of paving slabs for flooring

Using the domestic supply It could well be a practical proposition to run the conservatory heating direct from the domestic supply, but such a decision should be gone into carefully. Although there is the convenience of running the conservatory from the domestic supply, there is also a strong argument for an individual heating supply to the conservatory as it will be much simpler to control.

Hot water heating system In the days of the Victorians the conservatory and its nearby 'feeder' greenhouse would have been heated by a fairly substantial battery of hot water pipes connected to a solid fuel boiler. Even today the vast majority of commercial greenhouses are heated by circulation of hot water, with many of these establishments at present converting their oil-fired boilers to solid fuel. As oil prices are ever on the increase the principle reason for the change is to make the conservatory more economical to run.

Although the method of heating circulating water may vary, it is interesting to note that a piped hot water system for heating glassed-in areas is still considered to be the most effective, although the pipes and the plumbing for installing such systems has changed considerably from the four inch diameter cast iron heating pipes of the Victorian conservatory. Present systems will generally consist of small bore pipes with water being pumped under pressure to ensure that maximum efficiency is obtained.

Hot air fan system The conservatory that is heated by hot water pipes will have a much better feeling, a much better growing atmosphere if you like, than conservatories that are heated by other methods. Electrically operated hot air fans, for example, will inevitably create a dry atmosphere that will be alien to the majority of plants that one would expect to find in a well chosen conservatory collection. Although more costly to run as a sole means of heating; the electrically operated hot air fan can be extremely useful as a standby source of heating. Standby heating can be utilised in emergency, or to augment the main heat source when extreme weather conditions prevail.

Paraffin heating system Perhaps the least expensive method of heating both to install and to run will be paraffin units that are free standing and simple to maintain. However, if the plants in the conservatory are the principal concern it is advisable to acquire a paraffin heater that is specially designed for greenhouses as opposed to heaters that are intended for domestic use. In any event, when employing paraffin heaters it is extremely important that the unit should be regularly cleaned to ensure maximum efficiency, and further to ensure that at least one roof ventilator remains a fraction open so that any build up of toxic fumes can be avoided. You will find that there are a number of the more exotic plants that will deteriorate if exposed to the fumes of paraffin heaters for any length of time. If there is no alternative to paraffin as a means of heating the conservatory, it is wiser to experiment with smaller and less expensive plants than it is to introduce plants of specimen size, only to find that they are susceptible to the fumes of the paraffin heater.

Gas heating system In recent years there has been a marked increase in the use of gas heaters for smaller greenhouses and conservatories, and these are trouble free and take up very little floor space – the latter can be an important factor in smaller plant rooms. There is ever a fear on the part of the grower of potted plants in whatever environment, that gas spells death to his precious charges, and in the days of the Victorians this was indeed a matter for concern. However, with natural gas and much superior plumbing there is little reason for concern when heating premises by gas. Should there still be nagging doubts in spite of the assurances, one can test very simply for the presence of gas by employing gas-sensitive plants or flowers. In the presence of toxic gas fumes carnation flowers will keel over very rapidly, as will tomato plants – should tests with either of these prove positive it should be a natural step to pick up the telephone and call the Gas Company.

Emergency heating Perhaps the most basic form of heating is the very ordinary candle which comes into its own when the lighting fails indoors. Ability to provide a limited amount of light is one thing, but candles can also be utilised to provide a modest source of heat in emergency in the plant-filled conservatory. A dozen or so candles made secure in the bottom of a similar number of five inch diameter pots will offer a surprising degree of warmth. Clay pots are essential and it will be a further advantage if pots of similar diameter can be inverted over the pots in which the candles are burning.

Working out what capacity heater is needed
When the form of heating for the conservatory has been decided upon it will be necessary to take rough internal measurements of the building so that the supplier can be informed, in order that a heater of adequate capacity is obtained. It should also be borne in mind that there should be allowance for some reserve, as there is nothing worse than fighting the worst of the winter weather with a heating appliance that is not up to the task.

Conserving heat

The heaviest ongoing cost in managing the conservatory will be in heating, but if you wish to enjoy the pleasures of growing exotic plants, then heating is an inevitable part of the budget. During the summer months heating will only be necessary if more tender plants are being grown, and then only on colder nights. For this reason it will be a considerable advantage if the heating unit in the conservatory can be thermostatically controlled.

Being a high cost item one should make every effort to conserve as much heat as possible, and the first essential in this respect is to ensure that all doors, windows and ventilators are efficiently sealed. If the building is very tall it will be costly and unnecessary to heat the upper area, therefore the fitting of a false ceiling should be considered, and this can be simply achieved by stretching wires from one side of the room to the other so that a polythene, or thermal screen can be fitted to the wires to prevent heat loss. Polythene sheeting can also be put to use as an efficient form of winter double glazing that can be completely removed in early spring – insulation of this kind will save a full ten degrees of heat loss. Alternatively, roller blinds will save heat, be more attractive and can be additionally used as a form of shading during the summer months of the year.

In winter one should never be too anxious to open ventilators for other than short periods to admit a change of air and, in any event, vents should not remain open too late on winter afternoons as it is important to maximise as much as possible on the free heat of the sun if it is not to the detriment of the plants in the conservatory.

Ventilation

The conservatory must be adequately provided with ventilation – be it large windows or doors that can be fixed in the open position. Heating conservatories during the winter months can be a problem and a strain on the pocket very often, but it will be found that keeping the interior cool in summer is perhaps more difficult. Allowing a howling gale to blow through the leaves of your plants from every angle is not the answer, as such conditions can be more harmful than beneficial. Ventilators are generally opened on the lee side of the building, so all round ventilation should be the aim when choosing or constructing a conservatory. The doors of the structure can provide a useful source of air and, wherever possible, these should be located on the more sheltered side, or sides, of the building. North facing doors can be something of a problem during the winter months and will result in considerable heat loss. Fortunately, equipment is now available to provide automatic control over ventilators, which is much less tedious than having someone on hand to open and close vents manually. These are readily available from the garden sundriesman, or from the manufacturer of the conservatory. The alternative to this form of control is to have someone almost permanently on hand to operate ventilators as weather conditions fluctuate. One cannot place too much emphasis on the need for adequate ventilation

◀◀ *Flooring: Buff coloured ceramic tiles are used as decorative flooring in this sun lounge. Drainage should be provided.* (Smiths)

◀ *Flooring: Here a combination of ceramic tiles and carpet are used as flooring in this sun lounge which is used for eating in as well as providing a good environment for growing plants.* (W Davidson)

Ventilation: This older style conservatory has plenty of doors and windows that can be opened to let in air on hot days. (Bartholomew)

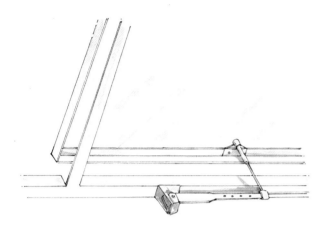

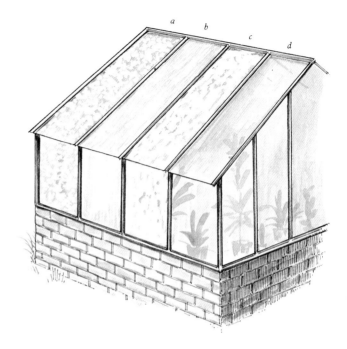

▲ *One type of automatic conservatory ventilator.*

▼ *Shading the conservatory by painting.*
a Dappled shade for early spring or for early-flowering plants (apply with syringe)
b Light-matt shading applied with a distemper brush, or can be fully syringed on.
c Heavy summer shading for foliage plants. Apply with a brush.
d Clear glass for winter and possibly cacti all year round.

▶ *Shading with blinds*

during the summer months and the larger and more numerous the windows the better the control one will have over the growing conditions. To ensure a good flow of air through the conservatory it will be an advantage if louvre windows can be fitted at lower level just above the brick foundations of the building. For openings at lower level it may be necessary to fit some form of mesh over the opening so that marauding animals can be kept out. Similar precautions may also be necessary if the door of the conservatory is to be allowed to stand open in order to admit fresh air.

Providing Shade

If plants are acquired during the summer months it will not be so important to provide heat, it will be more a question of combating heat that pours down from the sun. Almost all the plants that are offered by the retailer will have been cared for in large commercial greenhouses and almost all of these will have been shaded in some way to protect plants from the direct rays of the sun. Many plants, such as crotons, bougainvilleas and citrus, will tolerate a considerable amount of direct sunlight but even these will benefit from some protection if the sun is excessively hot. Green foliaged plants such as philodendrons will suffer considerably with full sun streaming through unprotected glass, and plants of the marantaceae family will simply curl up their leaves and die.

The simplest form of shading is to paint or spray on a shading material to the glass on the outside of the conservatory. This will ensure constant protection and may be almost suitable for a large expanse of glass, but it is not the most attractive method. Internal blinds can provide a more attractive alternative, and there is a wide range of colours and materials to choose from. Blinds also have the advantage that you do not have to have the plants shaded if the sun is not overhead, so offering plants lighter and better conditions in which to grow. But they also have the disadvantage of being manually operated which means that someone must be on hand to draw the blinds when the sun appears. Whatever form of shading one decides upon, the important thing to remember if plants are to succeed, is that protection from direct sunlight through clear glass is an absolute essential.

3 Filling the Conservatory with Plants

The interior of the conservatory that is used purely as a plant house should have a fullness about it when one enters the premises – plants ought to occupy every available space. Areas should be created so that one can use every corner and make possible the introduction of the maximum number of plants, so that a tropical garden effect is the result. There ought to be climbing plants, hanging plants, plants on shelves, plants on table staging and, for good measure, plants on the floor under the staging. Whatever else one learns about potted plants there is little doubt that they will do infinitely better if they are growing in the company of other plants rather than when dotted around in splendid isolation. Also, when thinly scattered around it is difficult to create a growing feeling in the conservatory, and without a moist and humid feeling in the conservatory there will be little hope of growing any of the more exotic plants very successfully. Even cacti that will tolerate all sorts of harsh treatment will improve both in appearance and performance if they can be grouped together rather than dotted around.

Buying Plants

Where do pests come from, is a question that is frequently asked by the person who is new to the growing of plants. Although they may come in at the window, the answer that is most often given to the question is that pests are in most instances purchased! They are bought with the plant from the retailer if

◀◀ *and* ◀ *Conservatories with plants occupying every available space.* (Smiths)

one is careless enough to select plants that are infested. There may be only a few pests on the plant of red spider, white fly or mealy bug when it is purchased but these are pests that will quickly increase in numbers in the agreeable conditions that exist in a properly run conservatory.

The lesson to be learned is that you should purchase plants from a known reliable source, and even then be wise enough to inspect the plant before any money changes hands. The majority of pests are found on the undersides of leaves or on the softer growing tips of such plants as impatiens, and a brief inspection will generally be sufficient to detect their presence. Pale, yellowish discolouration of leaves is often an indication that red spider mites are present on the plant so one should seek plants that are fresh green in appearance when making purchases. However, it must be added that coloured foliage plants, such as crotons and marantas, will provide very effective camouflage for these minute pests. Generally hardening of foliage and more stunted young shoots at the tops of stems will be a further sign that these mites are in attendance.

Purchased plants are generally free from pests and will grow to a high standard if plants are acquired from a reliable source, but it is, nevertheless, unwise to buy plants that are already in protective wrapping. A paper sleeve can conceal dead and dying leaves, therefore it is important that one should be able to inspect the entire plant for signs of indifferent culture. Quality plants will invariably be that little more expensive, but it is preferable to select the best possible quality when choosing plants to add to your collection.

Choosing Plants for Your Particular Conditions and Requirements

Before you rush out to stock your new conservatory, think carefully about the conditions in it. Is it shady or sunny? Is it a room as well as a home for tropical plants? Think about what effects you want to create

Inspecting a plant for pests.

in the conservatory. Do you want a background of climbing plants? Do you want plants hanging down in a series of hanging baskets? What about a water feature or a bromeliad tree? You can then write a list of plants to look for.

Plants for Different Light and Heat Conditions

If the conservatory is shaded and offers poor light, it is best to select plants with green foliage: *Rhoicissus rhomboidea*, *Aralia sieboldii* and a selection from the many philodendrons are good examples of the sort of plants to choose. More tender crotons and calatheas will require constant temperature and a degree of growing skill so it is advisable to leave those until one has acquired a degree of expertise. Seasonal flowering plants, begonias, fuchsias, geraniums and such like acquired in early spring and summer, will present few problems if one can offer good light and generally airy conditions with a modicum of care. However, when purchasing plants for winter flowering, poinsettias and cyclamen in particular, it will be necessary to provide reasonably warm conditions. For the poinsettia a minimum temperature of 60°F will be required, and for the cyclamen the temperature should not rise above this level. A partitioned conservatory offering two separate temperature regimes would be the answer for plants requiring temperatures of appreciable differences. For the enthusiast plantsman, a small partitioned area that is kept at higher temperature would be much more economical than having to heat the entire conservatory area because a few plants in the collection needed extra warmth.

Climbing Plants

There are many natural climbing plants that one can make excellent use of in the conservatory, some of these being dual purpose plants that will climb or trail depending on what is required of them – good examples in this respect are members of the araceae family, especially the smaller leaved philodendrons and the scindapsus. While some plants will climb naturally if provided with a framework, stephanotis and clerodendrons being good examples, it will be necessary actually to tie others to the framework.

Plants for a Bromeliad Tree

If there is sufficient space available, one of the most eye-catching plant arrangements that one can provide is a stout tree branch that is decorated with a selection of bromeliads. These plants have fascinating foliage, many with brilliant colouring, and flowers that are quite literally out of this world in exotic appearance. Yet they are among the easiest of plants to care for, being able to tolerate wide fluctuations in temperature, and quite long periods of drought conditions. However, they will give generally better performance if they are kept moist and if the temperature does not fall below 13°C/55°F.

The tree will be further enhanced by using smaller ferns as an alternative to bromeliads, and by employing smaller leaved trailing plants such as *Episcia dianthiflora* and *Ceropegia woodii*.

Bringing Plants Home

Having acquired your plants it would be very foolish simply to take them home and set them around in a brand new conservatory in the hope that they will flourish. If stocking of the area is being done during the winter it will clearly be essential to ensure that the interior of the building is adequately heated. Remember that delicate plants, such as calatheas, will die if exposed to cold conditions for the briefest of periods. Even when transporting plants from the heated premises of the supplier to your home it is important to ensure that plants are not exposed to cold conditions. For example, it can be fatal to place plants in the boot of a car over a lengthy journey in cold weather, as the boot area is very much colder than the area within the car, which can be heated.

On getting plants home, water the soil and then remove the plant from its pot so that the root development can be checked. If the plant is large in proportion to the size of the pot in which it is growing, and roots are very well developed it will be advisable to pot the plant on into a slightly larger container as soon as possible. A slightly larger container should be used for the step up, but never one of excessive size, and the soil should be a properly prepared houseplant mixture.

Better plant shops will carry a very wide range of both flowering and foliage pot plants, and if one is a beginner with these plants it is advisable to select those that are easier to manage. In fact, when seeking a large number of plants to stock a conservatory it will be advisable to get some professional advice from the person in charge of the plants rather than simply select plants at random.

Ananas (Smiths)

Nephrolepis exaltata (p. 32) (W Davidson)

Cacti (W Davidson)

4Gallery of Plants

Foliage Plants

Alocasia indica
Appearance: Arrow-shaped leaves. Blue green metallic colour.
Care notes: Keep moist. Temperature 18°C/65°F. Shade essential.
Position in conservatory: Pool margin ideal.

Asparagus Fern
A. plumosa
Appearance: Delicate, feathery foliage.
Care notes: Cool, shade, Peaty soil mixture.
Position in conservatory: Climber or trailer.
A. sprengeri
Appearance: Arching stems covered with thousands of short, flat needles.
Care notes: Very easy to grow in conservatory. Withstands most conditions.
Position in conservatory: Will clothe walls.

Aspidistra
Traditional Victorian conservatory plant.
Appearance: Spear-shaped, glossy leaves up to 50 cm (20 in) long.
Care notes: Very easy. Almost any conditions are suitable. Do not let soil become saturated over long periods of time.

Begonia
For beginner with conservatory plants: *B. haageana* (metallic green leaves).
Other good begonias for conservatories: *B. cleopatra* (small leaves), *B.heraclifolia* (large palmate leaves), *B. lucerne* (silver spotted leaves).
Care notes: Give good light but not direct sun. Temperature: 13–16°C/55–60°F. Very high temperatures detrimental. Peaty loam-based soil. With larger type plants pot on without delay. Keep moist and regularly fed while in active growth.
Problems: Mildew. Avoid dank conditions.

Bromeliads
Suitable varieties for conservatories:
Ananas (*A. comosus variegata*) (striking green and cream foliage, may develop a spectacular fruit in time.
Tillandsias, cryptanthus (star-shaped rosettes).
Care notes: Easy to care for. Avoid low temperatures and wet and cold conditions combined. Use peaty soil mixture. Protect from direct sunlight. See p. 56 for how to make a bromeliad tree.

Cacti
Suitable varieties for conservatories: *opuntias* and *mammilarias* (for beginners). Any other species can be grown.
Care notes: Give full light. Keep bone dry October–March. Begin to water in March and keep soil moist until October.

Calathea
Appearance: Beautiful mottled foliage in shades of green, grey and reddish brown. Try *C. makoyana*, *C. picturata* and *C. zebrina* or slightly easier

C. louisae, C. oppenheim and *C. ornata.*
Care notes: Difficult to care for. Minimum
temperature 18°C/65°F. Peaty soil. Never allow
to dry out.
Pests: Red spider mite in hot, dry conditions.
Place systemic insecticide in soil to protect plants.

Ceropegia (Hearts Entangled)
Appearance: Heart-shaped leaves on wiry
pendulous stems.
Care notes: Give good light. Do not let plants
become too wet. In winter water only once every
1–2 months.

Codieum (Croton)
Appearance: Upright habit. Narrow or broad
leaves in bright colours from yellow and orange to
deep red.
Care notes: Lightest possible location. Direct
sunlight beneficial but never allow soil to dry out
during summer and never to excess at any time.
Pests: Red spider mite. Treat with systemic
insecticide.

Cyperus
Varieties: *C. alternifolius* (2 m/8 ft tall), *C. diffusus*
(1 m/3–4 ft tall).
Appearance: Graceful grass. Slender upright stems
with umbrella tops.
Care notes: Must stand with roots in water. May
need canes to keep stems erect.
Position in conservatory: In pool.

Fatshedera
Appearance: Upright plant with large ivy-like
leaves.
Care notes: Good for cool conservatories. Only
needs 7–10°C/45–55°F.

Ferns

Adiantum (Maidenhair Fern)
Appearance: Slender stems. Delicate lacy fronds.
Care notes: Give shade, keep moist. Temperature
not less than 16°C/60°F.

Problems: Browning of fronds, often caused by
very wet and cold conditions. Drying up and
shrivelling – do not let soil dry out.

Nephrolepis exaltata (p. 30)
Appearance: Long erect fronds (up to 90 cm/3 ft).
Care notes: Peaty mixture. Semi-shade. Minimum
temperature 13°C/55°F.
Position in conservatory: Excellent in hanging
baskets.

Platycerium alcicorne (Stagshorn fern)
Appearance: Fronds like antlers. An epiphyte or
air plant.
Care notes: Minimum temperature 10°C/50°F.
Semi-shade. Plunge occasionally into a bucket of
water.
Position in conservatory: Good subject for
bromeliad tree.

Ficus
General care notes: Minimum temperature
16°C/60°F for *F. robusta*, 13°C/55°F for others.
Bright light. Water freely in summer, sparingly in
winter.
Ficus pumila (Creeping fig)
Appearance: Small pale green oval leaves. Stiff
arching stems.
Position in conservatory: Will climb damp walls
quickly.
Ficus robusta (Rubber plant)
Appearance: Bold, oval deep green leaves on
upright stems up to 2.5 m/8 ft tall.
Position in conservatory: In pots on floor.
Ficus benjamina (Weeping fig)
Varieties: *F.* 'Hawaii' and *F.* 'Golden Princess' (both
variegated).
Appearance: Glossy green oval leaves. Weeping
branches.
Care notes: Plenty of light. Protect from direct
sun.
Pests: Scale insects. Treat as soon as detected.

Ficus carica (Edible fig)
Appearance: This is the edible fig of commerce.

Care notes: Needs plenty of space. Two crops possible in conservatory, one on previous season's growth, one on current season's growth. Train branches to wall and along room. To avoid plants taking over, restrict roots to large pots. Water and feed regularly. Remove weak branches in spring.

Hedera (Ivies) p. 34
Care notes: Good for cool conservatories. Good light.
Position in conservatory: Good for hanging baskets or as climbers. Try *H. canariensis* (variegated) as tub plant or climber.

Heptapleurum (Parasol plant)
Good varieties: *H. capello* (golden with erect leaves)
Appearance: Fingered leaves on stiff petioles (like an umbrella).
Care notes: Easy to care for. Light shade. Keep moist. Temperature 16°C/60°F.

Maranta (Prayer plant)
Appearance: Low-growing plants with oval beautifully-coloured leaves.
Suitable varieties: *M. leuconeura kerchoveana* (pale green with dark green or maroon markings), *M. erythrophylla* (reddish green with bright red veining).
Care notes: Minimum temperature 10°C/50°F. Keep moist.
Position in conservatory: Good ground cover.

Monstera deliciosa (Swiss cheese plant)
Appearance: Large leaves, deeply cut and holed.
Care notes: Keep moist and warm (not less that 10°C/50°F in winter). Put aerial roots into containers of water. If plant becomes too tall, remove tops.

Musa cavendishii (Dwarf banana) (p. 34)
Appearance: Upright stem with large delicate oval leaves.
Care notes: Needs ample space but is more attractive when small. Minimum temperature 16°C/60°F. Likes hot conditions as long as it is moist.
Pests: Red spider mite.

Palms
Kentia forsteriana (Howea forsteriana)
Appearance: Feather-shaped leaves arch outwards from sturdy branches. Grows to 2-2.5 m/7-8 ft.
Care notes: Shade. Warmth (minimum temperature 10°C/50°F). Do not let soil dry out excessively.
Pests: Red spider mite. Treat with systemic insecticide.

Chamaedora elegans (Parlour palm)
Appearance: Smaller than *Kentia forsteriana* with fronds 30-60 cm (12-24 in) long. Best to buy 3 plants and pot them together.
Care notes: Keep moist at all times, but do not overwater.

Pandanus
Appearance: Strong prickly-edged leaves curving upwards in compact rosette. Grows to 2.5 m/10 ft or more.
Care notes: Needs a lot of space. Easy to care for. Good light, reasonable warmth (not less than 16°C/60°F) and soil that is never too wet.

Philodendron
General care notes: Water moderately. Mist foliage in summer. Minimum temperature 13-16°C/55-60°F. Shade from sun.
P. scandens (Sweetheart plant)
Appearance: Heart-shaped glossy leaves.
Care notes: Tolerant of poor light.
Position in conservatory: Good climber.
P. bipinnatifidum
Appearance: Leaves not impressive to start with but with adult foliage can become fine specimens. Forms a tree when mature and grows very big.
Care notes: Needs plenty of room.
P. hastatum
Appearance: Large arrow-shaped leaves.

Hedera 'Goldenchild' (p. 33) (W Davidson)

Pittosporum
Appearance: Masses of stiff, oval leaves. Colour according to variety.
Good varieties: *P. garnetti*, *P. usneoides* (grows to 2 m/8–9 ft).
Care notes: Plenty of light. Good for cooler conservatory.

Pleomele reflexa (Song of India)
Appearance: Rich golden leaves attached to stiff upright twisting stems. Leaves spiral round plant.
Care notes: Reasonable light. Temperature around 18°C/65°F. Water and feed carefully.

Rhoicissus
Appearance: Abundance of glossy green leaves about 5 cm/2 in long.
Care notes: Very easy. Objects to full sun. Minimum temperature 7°C/45°F.
Position in conservatory: Climber or trailer. Can be useful to cover ground in front of arrangements of taller plants, or can be grown on a support to provide a background for more colourful plants.

Sansevieria
Suitable varieties: *S. trisfasciata laurentii* (Mother-in-law's tongue), *S. hahnii* (good compact form).
Care notes: Water well, then allow to dry out before re-watering. No water or feed in winter.

Musa cavendishii (p. 33) (Smiths)

Pleomele reflexa 'Variegata' (Smiths)

Saxifrage (Mother of Thousands)
Appearance: Rounded hairy leaves. Greenish brown mottled colour. Develops runners with miniature plants on the end.
Care notes: Bright light away from direct sunlight. Dryish soil. Temperature: Cool to average.
Position in conservatory: Good in hanging baskets.

Schefflera (Umbrella Plant)
Appearance: Bold, upright-growing green plants with green finger leaves on stout petioles.
Care notes: Minimum temperature 13°C/55°F. Light shade. Keep moist. Feed in spring and summer.

Scindapsus (Devil's Ivy)
Appearance: Attractive yellowish foliage mottled with green. Similar to a philodendron scandens.
Care notes: Warm, humid, shady conditions.
Position in conservatory: Good climber or trailer.

Senecio
Appearance: Small leaves. Looks a bit like ivy.
Care notes: Good light. Do not overwater.
Position in conservatory: Good climber.

Sparmannia africana (Wind flower)
Appearance: Pale green vine-like leaves. White flowers with prominent stamens in summer.

Care notes: Bright light out of direct sun. Minimum temperature 7°C/45°F. If fed and properly cared for, will grow very fast.

Succulents
General care notes: Water very sparingly in winter. Full light. Do not put into pots too large for their size.
Echeveria
Appearance: Neat rosettes of fleshy leaves, overlapping at base. Various colours. Metallic grey particularly attractive. Dainty pink flowers.
Sedum morganianum (Burro's tail)
Appearance: Blue-grey fleshy leaves attached to pendulous stems. Looks like plaits.

Tetrastigma
Appearance: Rampant-growing foliage plant.
Care notes: Easy to care for. Minimum temperature 13°C/55°F. Feed and water frequently. Large pots and frames will be needed.
Position in conservatory: Climber, or place on a pillar so plant is forced to be a trailer.

Vines
Care notes: Good for cool, airy conservatories. Consult your nurseryman for advice on obtaining vines. Plant out in spring outside conservatory with shoots going through a hole in the wall into

Sparmannia africana (Smiths)

Vine (in the conservatory at Hampton Court) (E Saqui)

the building. Attach stem to supports. Thin growth throughout summer. At end of season, cut back shoots branching off main stem to two eyes. Thin branches of grapes so that good size fruit is produced. Keep training wires well away from wall. Plant in good turfy loam with bone meal added. Feed well.

Yucca
Appearance: Woody stem topped with spiky clusters of long stiff green leaves.
Care notes: Easy to care for. Good light. Minimum temperature 7°C/45°F. Let soil dry out between waterings.

Flowering Plants

Acacia (p. 38)
Appearance: Soft delicate leaves similar to ash in shape. Trusses of yellow flowers in spring.
Care notes: Plant directly into the soil. Keep moist and fed. High temperature not necessary.
Position in conservatory: Background for other colourful plants.

Achimenes
Appearance: Dull unattractive foliage but beautiful brightly-coloured flowers.
Care notes: Start rhizomes in February by plunging briefly into hot water before planting. Keep moist and fed. Modest temperature.
Position in conservatory: Good in hanging baskets at shoulder height to display flowers.

Aeschynanthus lobbiana
Appearance: Dark green pendulous foliage. Cupped deep red flowers.
Care notes: Very easy. Keep moist, fed and in shade. Minimum temperature 16°C/60°F.

Allamanda
Appearance: Spectacular large yellow trumpet flowers in summer.
Care notes: Feed well while in active growth.

Loam-based soil. Keep warm and moist. Prune hard in autumn.

Anthurium (p. 38)
Appearance: A. scherzerianum (short leathery leaves, bright red flowers). A. andreanum (arrow-shaped leaves. Many colours for flowers).
Care notes: Minimum temperature 16°C/60°F. Moist, humid, shade. Peaty soil. Do not let soil get excessively wet.

Aphelandra squarrosa Louisae
Appearance: Green leaves with bright silver markings. Yellow long-lasting bracts in mid summer.
Care notes: Abundant moisture. Feed roots. Minimum temperature 16°C/60°F. Protect from direct sun. Rich potting mixture. Check plants do not become pot bound.

Azalea indica
Appearance: Small rounded dark green leaves. Flowers in many colours from winter to spring.
Care notes: Keep out of doors in summer after flowering, and keep very moist and well fed. Remove dead flowers after flowering. Keep cool and light (7–16°C/45–60°F).

Begonia
Tuberous-rooted
Care notes: Start tubers in boxes of warm peat in February. When well sprouted, transfer to pots. Rich potting mixture. Feed well, keep moist. Good light.
Fibrous-rooted
Care notes: Good light. Good air circulation.
Position in conservatory: Many pendulous begonias are good in hanging baskets.
Problems: Mildew – use Benlate fungicide if attack is mild. Destroy plant if bad.

Beloperone
Varieties: B. guttata (Shrimp plant) (reddish brown bracts), B. guttata lutea (yellow bracts).
Care notes: Good light. Feed well. Keep moist.

Bougainvillea (p. 38)
Appearance: Spectacular plants with brilliantly-coloured paper thin bracts.
Care notes: Full light. Water and feed well when growing. When foliage is shed in autumn do not feed or water. Keep bone dry over winter and minimum temperature 7–10°C/45–50°F.
Position in conservatory: Climber or train on frame in a pot.

Bulbs
Preparation: Plant in August/September. 'Crock' pots and use loam-based soil to cover crocks. Plant one or two layers of bulbs, then cover bulbs completely with soil about 2.5 cm/1 in from rim of pot. Place pots in cold frame covered with 10 cm/4 in sand. When tips show, lift pots and take into conservatory.

Callistemon (Bottle brush)
Appearance: Hard woody stems. Thin linear leaves. Red brush-like flowers.
Care notes: Easy to care for. Loam-based soil. Do not overwater.

Camelia
Appearance: Rich glossy green foliage. Single and double flowers in many colours in spring.
Care notes: Unheated conservatory. Acid soil. Water with rain water.

Campanula isophylla
Appearance: Hard green foliage. Small white or blue bell flowers in summer.
Care notes: Light and cool (7–10°C/45–50°F). Remove dead flowers. Prune back old stems after flowering. Store over winter. Water sparingly.
Position in conservatory: Hanging basket.

Cineraria
Appearance: Annuals with bright daisy flowers in spring in many colours.
Care notes: Cool, light with plenty of food and water.
Pests: Many. Keep careful watch.

Clerodendron
Appearance: Red and white flowers on woody stems in summer. Coarse green leaves.
Care notes: Minimum temperature 16°C/60°F. Older plants shed leaves so always have younger plants to replace them. Water and feed well when growing. Water sparingly and do not feed in winter.

Citrus Mitis (Orange tree) (P. 38)
Appearance: Small green oval leaves. Scented white flowers. Small bitter oranges. Grows 60–100 cm/2–3 ft tall.
Care notes: Quite difficult to grow. Keep out of doors in summer, indoors in winter. Temperature 13–15°C/55–60°F in winter. Water almost daily in summer, every 10 days in winter. Do not like being waterlogged. Mist every day. Loam-based soil.

Clivia miniata (Kaffir lily)
Appearance: Long strap-like leaves. No stalk. Rich orange flowers.
Care notes: Warm (5–10°C/40–50°F), moist shade. Easy to care for.

Columnea banksii
Appearance: Oval-shaped evergreen foliage on stout pendulous stems. Brilliant orange flowers in spring.
Care notes: Keep moist, well fed and shaded. Keep dryish December–early January.
Position in conservatory: Hanging basket.

Cyclamen (p. 39)
Appearance: Green rounded leaves marked with silver. Butterfly flowers in shades of white – deep pink.
Care notes: Do not let roots become waterlogged. Water frequently but let dry out between waterings. Store plant dry until new leaves evident. Then water and re-pot.
Position in conservatory: Grow in adjacent greenhouse and take into conservatory to provide splash of brightness when at peak.

Acacia baileyana (p. 36) (Smiths)

Anthurium andreanum (p. 36) (Smiths)

Bougainvillea 'Miss Manila Hybrid' (p. 37) (Smiths)

Citrus mitis (p. 37) (Smiths)

Mini cyclamen (p. 37) (Smiths)

Dipladenia splendens (p. 40) (Smiths)

Gardenia (p. 40) (Smiths)

Hoya carnosa (p. 40) (Smiths)

Dipladenia sanderi 'Rosea' (p. 39)
Appearance: Delicate climbing foliage with pink bell flowers.
Care notes: Moist, warm shade. Minimum temperature 13°C/53°F. Peaty potting mixture.
Position in conservatory: Climber.

Episcia dianthiflora
Appearance: Naturally pendulous stems with clusters of pale green leaves and white flowers with frilled edges.
Care notes: Easy to care for. Bright light. Minimum temperature 13°C/55°F.

Euphorbia pulcherrima (Poinsettia)
Appearance: Brightly coloured bracts.
Care notes: Peaty mixture. To encourage plants to flower in November/December, allow no artificial light in evening. Water thoroughly but reduce amount during rest period.

Fuchsia
Appearance: Pendulous flowers in many colours in single or double forms. Upright and pendulous forms and standards. Flowers from spring to autumn.
Care notes: Good light. Airy conditions. Peaty soil. Feed well and keep moist.

Gardenia (p. 39)
Appearance: Glossy dark green foliage. Scented beautiful flowers.
Care notes: Difficult to grow. Minimum temperature 16°C/60°F. Maximum temperature 21°C/70°F. Keep soil moist but avoid long periods of saturation and drought conditions.
Problems: Yellow foliage – treat with Iron Sequestrene. Flower buds fall off – do not let temperature or water fluctuate.

Gloriosa
Appearance: Similar to lilies. Red and yellow colours with prominent stamens.
Care notes: Plant tubers in pots of peaty soil in

February. Minimum temperature 16°C/60°F. Bright light.

Hibiscus rosa sinensis
Appearance: Bright flowers in many colours from spring to autumn.
Care notes: Good light. Moist, airy conditions. Minimum temperature 13°C/55°F.
Pests: Red spider. Mealy bug.

Hoya (p. 39)
Hoya carnosa
Appearance: Climbing tendrils with pendulous clusters of waxy flowers.
Hoya bella
Appearance: Compact plant with brittle stems and marvellous jewel flowers. For hanging baskets.
Care notes: Minimum temperature 16°C/60°F. Keep moist, fed and out of direct sun.
Pests: Red spider.

Jasminum polyanthum
Appearance: Semi-evergreen climber with scented small star-like white flowers (November–April). Few plants are better in a conservatory for quickly covering walls.
Care notes: Cool temperature (13°C/55°F). Keep moist and mist leaves frequently.
Position in conservatory: Plant in ground. Climber.

Lapageria
Appearance: Exquisite elongated bell flowers. Plants difficult to obtain.
Care notes: Pot in large containers. Loam-based compost with lots of peat and grit. Cool temperature.

Medinilla
Appearance: Naturally pendulous blooms.
Care notes: Keep moist and feed well in summer. Do not feed in winter. Minimum temperature 18°C/65°F. Ample space needed for spreading growth and pedestal on which to place plants in flower.

Orchids

Care notes: Best to segregate tender orchids in a warmer and humid section at one end of the conservatory (see page 29). For the beginner it is best to start with such as cymbidiums.

Cymbidiums

Appearance: Strap leaves. Flowers spring direct from bulb. Long-lasting flowers in many colours.
Care notes: Good light (at least 10–15 hours a day). Cool, airy conditions. Special orchid potting mixture.

Passiflora caerulea (Passion flower)

Appearance: Sprawling unattractive growth. Intricate flowers predominantly blue in colour.
Care notes: Good sunny light. Feed and water well. Keep compost moist. Temperature 5–10°C/40–50°F in winter.
Position in conservatory: Climber. Give a support.

Pelargonium (Geranium)

Appearance: Many different varieties and colours available for potted plants and hanging baskets.
Care notes: Easy to care for. Good sunny light. Plenty of fresh air. Reduce watering in winter. Compost should be barely moist.

Plumbago (Cape leadwort) (p. 43)

Appearance: Clusters of sky blue (*P. capensis*) or white (*P. capensis alba*) flowers on rambling stems through summer and autumn.
Care notes: Good for cool conservatories. Minimum temperature 7°C/45°F. Bright light with protection from strong direct sun. Keep moist. Water sparingly in winter. Mist occasionally. Loam-based soil. Grows fast. Prune shoots back to base after flowering. Keep on the dry side over winter but water and feed well at other times.
Position in conservatory: Climber.

Saintpaulia (African Violet) (p. 42)

Appearance: Small round hairy leaves with bright flowers in many colours.
Care notes: Grow on benching with capillary matting or stand the pots on pebble-filled trays. Minimum temperature 16°C/60°F. Protect from strong sunlight. Peaty potting mixture. When watering, avoid getting water on leaves. Give enough water each time to see water drain out from bottom of pot. Let soil dry out between waterings. Feed well. Remove dead flowers and leaves as soon as seen.

Schlumbergera (Christmas Cactus)

Appearance: Flowers in late November.
Care notes: Easy to care for. Good light. Peaty soil. Do not allow to become excessively wet. Place out of doors in summer.
Problems: Bud drop – do not move plants once buds have formed.

Sinningia (Gloxinia)

Appearance: Large, ungainly leaves radiating from corm with brightly-coloured trumpet flowers in summer.
Care notes: Light location. Feed and water well when growing. Keep dormant corm dry and warm over winter.

Spathiphyllum

Appearance: Large dark green leaves emerge from soil on firm stalks. White spathe flowers at intervals throughout year.
Care notes: Semi-shade. Moist. Minimum temperature 13°C/55°F. Keep compost moist and mist leaves frequently. Peaty soil.

Stephanotis (Madagascar Jasmine) (p. 42)

Appearance: Natural climber with evergreen leathery leaves. White tubular flowers with star-like ends borne in clusters. Very fragrant. Grows fast.
Care notes: Good light, but not full sun. Keep moist and feed in spring and summer. Do not feed, and water sparingly in winter. Temperature 13–16°C/55–60°F.
Position in conservatory: Climber. Provide frame.

Streptocarpus (Cape primrose) (p. 42)

Appearance: Brittle green leaves with rough

Saintpaulia, mixed (p. 41) (Smiths)

Stephanotis floribunda (p. 41) (Smiths)

Streptocarpus 'Diana' (p. 41) (Smiths)

▶ *Plumbago capensis* (with sesbania) (p. 41) (Smiths)

surface sprout from soil level. Flowers in many
colours will last many months.
Care notes: Best to acquire plants at beginning of
summer. Good light. Moisture. Peaty soil mixture.

Velthemia
Appearance: Rosettes of pale green leaves with
pink, brush-like flowers in summer.
Care notes: Keep moist and fed. Loam-based soil.

5 Effective Display

It is even more important to display plants well in the conservatory than it is in the house, because here the plants are the main focus of attention. A really well designed conservatory can look spectacular and the choice of attractive garden furniture can add to the effect.

The best looking conservatories have plant interest at all levels: spectacular climbing background plants, hanging baskets containing colourful trailing plants, plant-filled tables and shelves at different levels, and plants growing from floor level. One of the most attractive features in a conservatory, if you can afford it, is a water garden. The sight of water seems to have a calming, restful effect on most people.

Displaying Climbing Plants

If the conservatory has the outside wall of the house as one of its sides, then this wall should be put to full use for accommodating climbing plants, and there are many both easy and difficult plants to choose from. The roots of plants growing against the wall can be restricted to a container. This can be an advantage for such vigorous plants as the Passion Flower, or they can be free planted in the soil on which the conservatory is standing. In the latter case it will be important to improve the soil by incorporating a liberal amount of peat and by adding a general fertiliser such as Growmore.

Trellises Before planting climbing plants, one should be optimistic enough to provide an adequate framework to which plants can be trained, or on which they can climb naturally if that should be their habit. A visit to the garden sundriesman will show that they stock a wide range of products that may be utilised as plant climbing frames. Flexible plastic-covered wire mesh comes in rolls of varying width and will probably be the most economical material to purchase. It also has the advantage of being reasonably attractive and very easy to handle. The mesh can be attached flush to the wall by using screws or special nails for driving into masonry. Alternatively, the mesh can be set to stand proud of the wall by some three to four inches, so that plants climbing against and around it will have a more pleasing and less cramped appearance.

For better appearance there is the additional possibility of providing either metal or timber trellis work to which plants can be attached. If such trellis has a white finish it will considerably enhance the interior of the conservatory, and plants with green foliage will be seen to better advantage when placed against it. Although trellis of this kind can very easily be acquired ready-assembled, it is also possible to purchase the necessary materials so that trellis can be made to your own requirements. Trellis made in this way can be so designed that it will fit around corners, over doorways and such like.

In larger conservatories trellis work can be utilised to sub-divide the interior of the room, and such trellis can be very effective if made in a square pattern rather than the more conventional diamond shape. Trellis that is away from the wall can be suspended from the ceiling or, perhaps more effectively, it can be provided with free-standing legs that will permit one to re-locate the framework and attached plants as

◀ *Bougainvillea*, one of the most exotic and spectacular climbing plants. (Smiths)

▲ *A trellis is used to train greenery, a background for colourful begonias.* (E Slade)

and when required. Portable trellis features of this kind will obviously need to have plants growing alongside in containers that can be moved without too much difficulty when the trellis is moved to a fresh location.

Greenery can very often make an effective background for colourful plants, and there are numerous natural climbing plants that can be used for this purpose. Of these the Grape Ivy, *Rhoicissus rhomboidea* and its very similar counterpart, *Rhoicissus* 'Ellendancia', are ideal for the purpose of climbing and clothing an internal wall in a comparatively short space of time. Both these plants are tough subjects that will tolerate difficult conditions and they are also natural climbers with lots of clinging tendrils.

There are also numerous more upright growing philodendrons with interesting leaf shapes and colouring that could be pressed into service for the purpose of covering a trellis placed against a wall. Unless the wall is very wet, which is highly unlikely, these are not self-clinging plants and would have to be trained into the desired position as they increased

in size. The Sweetheart Plant, *P. scandens*, has small heart-shaped leaves that are green in colour, and has been well proven over the years as a durable indoor plant, so should not present any difficulties. With larger leaves and slightly more tender there is *P. burgundy* which, as the name suggests, has reddish coloured foliage.

In the more colourful range of exotic plants that can be induced to climb perhaps the best known is the bougainvillea which is so much part of the tropical holiday scene. If the conservatory offers good light, this is a fine plant to consider and is not as difficult to manage as one is sometimes given to believe. There are numerous varieties to choose from, but larger plants (the sort that would be required) tend to be scarce, so would need searching out. The bougainvillea is not a natural climber, so would have to be tied into position.

For heady fragrance and natural ability to climb any available support there is probably no plant that can match the stephanotis, *S. floribunda*, which has glistening white flowers that are formed in neat clusters emanating from the base of the leaf where it is attached to the main stem. The leaves are of leathery texture and oval in shape, and the plants climb in much the same way as runner beans with main stems entwining any available support.

Less usual as a climbing plant is *Clerodendron thompsonae* which has twining stems and coarse green leaves that are not in themselves very appealing, but the plant's main feature are the large clusters of red and white bracts that appear throughout the summer months. It is a plant that is becoming more readily available at plant centres, but it does need temperature of around 18°C/65°F and careful watering and feeding in order to do well.

Hanging Baskets and Trailing Plants

Within the conservatory one should never forget that an important aspect of display is change, change that will mean moving plants and props around so that the interior of the conservatory may acquire a fresh look. Any display of plants that is left in the same position for too long will inevitably take on a drab appearance that is much less effective than the collection of plants that is periodically cleaned over and rearranged.

Likewise, plants that are suspended from the roof of the conservatory will present another dimension that will add much to the general appearance of the plants that are on display. Although plants may be grouped together to create an effect it will be found that for more permanent display effect it is preferable to utilise plants as individuals in hanging containers. For this purpose, plants such as *Columnea, Episcia dianthiflora* and *Ceropegia woodii* are excellent as they are easy to care for and may remain in the same containers for several years if watering and feeding is attended to.

For the location that offers good light, one of the most attractive of basket plants is the humble *Campanula isophylla* which is available in both blue and white colouring. The foliage is not especially attractive, but when properly grown it will develop

trails four to five feet in length with so many flowers in evidence that the foliage is barely visible. Dead flowers should be regularly picked off and when plants have completed their flowering for the season in early autumn one can be quite savage and cut everything back almost to the rim of the container. Thereafter, the plant is kept just ticking over until the following spring when it can be watered and re-potted in the same container, having first removed much of the old soil from around the roots.

In the family acanthaceae there are many spectacular flowering plants for the conservatory that can withstand reasonably cool conditions – minimum of 13°C/55°F. One of the easiest plants in the family to care for is *Columnea banksii*, which has small, oval-shaped evergreen leaves that may trail for a yard or more, and fascinating orange flowers in January, lasting through to the end of March. With brighter flowers and much smaller leaves, *C. microphylla* is a little more difficult to care for, but when well grown is capable of producing trailing stems that may be six feet or more in length.

Traditional wire hanging baskets can be used for planting if they are first lined with moss (sphagnum moss of good quality is essential) and are then filled with appropriate potting mixture before plants are introduced. Such baskets vary in size and the dimension of the basket will to some degree dictate the number and size of plants that may be put in the container. However, having mentioned the possibility of using moss-lined wire baskets, it must be said that these are not entirely suitable for internal use as it is inevitable that when watering the basket the surplus will drain through and splash onto the floor or plants that may be underneath. If mess of this kind is not a problem then all is well, but it will usually be found that mossed baskets are really better suited to outside use, and can be very spectacular when utilised as an extension to the conservatory by suspending them on the outside wall where there is usually an attractive patio feature linking the conservatory to the garden.

As the fashion for hanging plants has increased over the years so the range of containers for accommodating them has also been greatly improved. Use of plastic containers in connection with indoor plants is often frowned upon, but there are numerous hanging baskets and planters of excellent design, and in assorted colouring that will set off plants to good effect. To avoid the problem of having drips falling from containers suspended overhead many of these units have drip trays that clip neatly onto the base of the container for catching surplus water. Excellent though these are they can cause problems when surplus water lying in the tray is subsequently drawn back into the soil by capillary action, so resulting in plants becoming much too wet. Ideally, one should water these containers and allow about half an hour to elapse before tilting the container to one side so that the surplus water may be disposed of.

The alternative to plastic is to use containers that are made from natural materials, and it must be said that plants will almost invariably be more attractive when such materials are used when presenting them in a display situation. String hangers, made of Macra né, have come a long way in recent years and are now available in an incredible assortment of designs from the very plain to the very elaborate. Most of these are designed to accommodate a pot or planter of some kind or other, or they may be large enough to accept a lightweight cane-type table top. The latter can be effective when supporting a collection of plants at lower level where they can be handled and seen to maximum effect.

Macramé hangers are usually seen to best effect, however, when they are supporting individual or multi pots of attractive design. Some of the best plants for these containers are the ones that can be induced to both climb and trail, with the result that some parts of the plants will entwine and climb the string support while other sections of the plant can be allowed to hang naturally. Plants ideally suited for this purpose would include examples of the many fine ivies, the Grape Ivy, *Rhoicissus rhomboidea* and the Sweetheart Plant, *Philodendron scandens*.

Having a collection of plants hanging in the conservatory in all sorts of odd locations can in some circumstances be very effective, while in other areas it may be little more than an untidy clutter. To overcome the latter problem it will frequently be more effective, certainly easier to manage, if all the

hanging plants are grouped in one section to form a dominant feature. To hang lots of plants in straight lines that follow the structural lines of the conservatory can be very dull. In similar fashion a collection of plants that are all suspended at the same height can be less effective than the same collection of plants that are at staggered levels.

A simple and effective way of overcoming this problem is to acquire a section of weldmesh, about 10×7.5 cm (4×3 in) and to suspend this from the ceiling, ensuring that it is well secured. It will then be a simple matter to hook hanging containers into the squares of the weld mesh so that complete flexibility of location becomes possible. To get over the problem of having all containers suspended at the same level one can use clear fishing line to extend the length of the hanging support so that an interesting collection of assorted plants at varying levels can be achieved. A collection of different ivies and different ferns used in conjunction with one another can be extremely effective when presented as a collection in this way. One need not always have the most exotic of plants to obtain an interesting and appealing effect. Similarly, a collection of impatiens grouped with an assortment of tradescantias will provide a fine display that will be little bother to care for.

Wall Mounted Containers

Many of the conservatory plants, even those that are not naturally trailing, or pendulous, will be seen to very good effect when placed in wall mounted containers. These can be attached to any wall or supporting post in the conservatory but, because they dry out very quickly they are not well suited to exposed, sunny locations.

Table Staging

If one is interested in the widest possible selection of plants it will be necessary to grow most of those in smaller pots in order to accommodate the greatest variety. To scatter small pots around on the floor of

A plastic hanging basket suitable for the conservatory.

the conservatory would be quite impractical, therefore some form of table staging is required on which plant pots can be placed and cared for without too much inconvenience. At floor level, plants will generally be in cooler temperature, so it is advantageous to raise them to slightly higher level if only to get better growth as a result of the higher temperature that will prevail. Aluminium materials are neat and strong, and it will not be difficult to locate sources of supply by scanning the advertisements of almost any gardening weekly. If one has the necessary skills it will be possible to construct staging from other materials. When completed, the top of the staging should have a two-inch thickness of gravel or similar material that will retain moisture, placed on top of the staging. Plants in pots that rest on such material will grow very much better as a result of the moisture that is retained in the material used to cover the staging.

Floor Level Plants

At floor level in the conservatory there are all sorts of possibilities in connection with display. You may want to plant some plants in the soil itself. In this case, when the flooring material is being laid you should decide which areas will be most suitable for a display of plants so that the particular spot is not slabbed, tiled or whatever. The area can be dug out and filled in with a good potting soil and then planted with a selection of plants.

The area can be planted conventionally, or it can be done with hydroculture plants, or plants in half-hydro as described elsewhere. Both the last mentioned methods of growing will reduce the need for everyday feeding and watering.

Any form of permanent planting within the conservatory is an important decision to make because one will have to live with it. Often the best approach is to set out the plants in their pots initially and to live with them for a few days, altering them around if necessary. After a little time you get to know what is right and can make the decision that that is how they should be planted.

▲ *Azaleas on table staging.* (Jacobs)
▶ *Pot plants on table staging and on floor level.* (Smiths)

50

Plants for Conservatories which are also Extra Rooms

Where plants are only part of the scene and are having to compete with tables, chairs and other accoutrements for space, it is usually advisable that they be placed around the walls or in free-standing containers that can be moved from one location to another without too much difficulty. Should flexibility be a factor when arranging plants for the conservatory it is well worth having a look at some of the self-watering containers that have castors fitted to their base to make re-location a simple task. However, it must be said that to be forever wheeling plants about from one area to another can be detrimental, as they barely get time to adjust to one growing station when they are on their way to the next.

An advantage of these office-type containers, that are intended for more or less permanent sites within the conservatory, is that the right sort of plants can be selected for filling them. If the location is light and offering some sunlight then plants such as crotons can be employed, whereas if the position is more in the shade then plants that prefer such conditions can be chosen. If the position is likely to be very hot and dry then there is no reason why the container should not be planted up with a selection of cacti which will be in their element in full sun.

When planting containers, one should seek a good balance and choose plants that will be reasonably harmonious in respect of colouring. Naturally it will also help if they require similar light conditions, and will not be too much at odds in respect of watering and feeding. With such containers it will also be found that much better results will be achieved if mature and well established plants are selected and planted rather than to plant up a greater number of tiny plants. The latter are much less imposing in larger containers and invariably do less well than established plants in similar conditions. Whatever sorts of plants may be used it is important that the soil in the pot is well watered and that the soil in which they are to be planted is moist, before anything else is done.

Office type containers are convenient and can be grouped to make effective displays. They are particularly useful where carpet is used as flooring.

If containers are filled with soil and planted conventionally, at least six months should elapse before any feeding is done, and plants can go for several years before disturbance for potting is considered. These larger containers that are principally used for interior landscaping can also be planted up with hydroculture plants, in which case they can go on almost indefinitely without disturbance if nutrients are provided according to directions that will come with the special fertiliser that is required when growing plants in water only. Containers may also be planted in the half-hydro fashion, and will need the same attention for feeding as plants being grown in a full hydroculture system.

There are all sorts of options open once the conservatory is constructed and plants are being introduced. Complicated though they appear, the various methods of growing plants can add considerably to the overall interest.

Water Features

If added public interest is anything to go by there is little doubt that any plant display that incorporates water as part of the feature will attract a great deal of attention. Water can be incorporated in all sorts of ways, and it would seem that in large areas the more noise and disturbance there is from splashing water then the more the onlooker is likely to enjoy the spectacle. Within the confines of a conservatory the continual sound of noisily gushing water can become more than a little disconcerting in time, so it is not a very practical proposition. But a gentle spray of water, or water falling into a pool in similar fashion to droplets of rain can have a very soothing and pleasing effect. Pools can be made with thick waterproof sheeting, or they may be purchased ready for placing in position, but whatever is decided upon it should be borne in mind that the pool feature should not be too substantial and permanent at the outset. Permanent features are fine until one tires of them and then has the task of removing them.

Making a pool from bricks and waterproof sheeting.

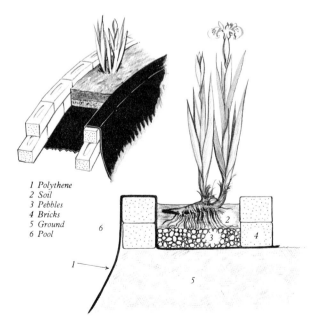

1 Polythene
2 Soil
3 Pebbles
4 Bricks
5 Ground
6 Pool

A conservatory can be used as a sunny extra room for eating in and relaxing. (Bartholomew)

In this sun lounge the wooden furniture blends well with the timber frame and flooring. (Bartholomew)

A small sun lounge, used as a study and relaxation room is enlivened by a spectacular corner display of mainly foliage plants.

Initially it is much better to do something simple and to get the feel of it before deciding to get the local builder in to cement together a permanent feature. A temporary and quite adequate pool can be made by arranging two rows of bricks and lining the area with waterproof sheeting. A further row of bricks can then be placed on top of the existing bricks with the sheeting in between. To prevent the weight of water pushing the bricks out of position a further circle of bricks, two bricks high, can be placed around the original bricks and the intervening space can be filled with peat into which a selection of plants can be placed. The surplus sheeting can be covered neatly by the peat and plants can be plunged to their rims in the peat to give a very attractive water garden feature. A pump and fountain will complete the picture, and one will have the satisfaction of knowing that it can all be very easily removed if space is needed for other purposes, or simply if one tires of the scene. Never forget that change is a very important aspect of display.

Making a Bromeliad Tree

A bromeliad tree can be used to best effect in the conservatory if it is combined with a water feature, and allowed to hang over a pool.

The initial step when contemplating such a feature in the conservatory is to select a sound tree branch with firm, rather than flimsy, projecting arms. The branch should be placed upright or at a slight angle in the position that one anticipates will be the final one. Then most of the secondary branches should be removed so that only four or five of the firmer and more interesting ones are left. As the branch has to be firmly anchored it may be necessary to provide it with a concrete base in which to embed the lower end of the main stump. This can be easily done by placing the tree in a large pot or a cut-down five-gallon drum. Use bricks to hold it in a central position before pouring in concrete which will make a heavy and firm base.

Lengths of half inch diameter hosepipe are then attached to the bare branches, ensuring that the lower end is reasonably long for the purposes of attaching a water pump. One can easily obtain hose fittings that will make it a simple operation to distribute the water supply from the central section of the hosepipe to the pipes that are fixed to the branches.

The most tedious, albeit one of the most important aspects of the exercise is then to cover the entire tree with fresh, good quality sphagnum moss – the fresher and better the quality, the better the final appearance of the tree will be. Use plastic-covered wire, which is more rust resistant, and ensure a good thickness of moss which should be tied around the branches securely. Surprisingly, the easiest part of the operation is the planting, but one should avoid the temptation to overdo this aspect.

Plants should be chosen carefully, selecting large or small objects depending on the overall size of the tree. Bromeliads will be the mainstay, and by shopping around one will be able to acquire a good selection of plants. Smaller plants could come from the cryptanthus and tillandsia genus, with *Tillandsia usneoides*, Spanish Moss, being an important acquisition. The latter is a suffocating weed in tropical America, but when the grey, mossy growth is suspended from a tree in the conservatory it can be a very attractive plant, and requires virtually no attention other than moisture and warmth. There are numerous larger bromeliads to choose from and these are seen at their best when located at the intersection of larger branches on the tree.

Smaller orchids will also do much to enhance the overall appearance of the tree, even if it means removing them after they have flowered so that they can be replaced with more colourful plants. Although colour is perhaps the most important requirement, one should not forget that an element of greenery will set off more colourful plants to better advantage, and the best plants for this purpose are the smaller and more compact ferns, of which there are many. Humble plants will also play a part: ivies, chlorophytum, *Episcia dianthiflora* and such like.

Before attaching them to the tree, plants are removed from their pots, having had a good watering, and roots are then covered with a good layer of moss which is wired into position. The moss virtually takes

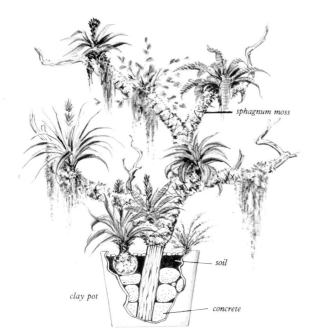

sphagnum moss

soil

clay pot

concrete

A bromeliad tree

the place of the pot and the ball is secured to the tree in what one considers to be the most favourable position. The finished tree will have to be kept moist by daily spraying over, with the occasional liquid feed used as an alternative to clear water.

When all is set up, the lower end of the hosepipe is attached to a small capacity pump. Block off the opposite ends of the pipe and perforate it at intervals along its length (small holes are quite adequate) after fixing it to the tree. This should give a gentle, soothing and very pleasing ripple on the pool below from the raindrops above!

Lighting Effects

Probably the time when the conservatory is most likely to be viewed is in the evening, so it is important to choose effective lighting. It is now possible to obtain lighting that is specially manufactured for the benefit of indoor plants, although some of these lights give some plants unnatural colouring. If desired, warm white strip lighting can be employed and will benefit the growth of plants as well as improving their general appearance. Spot lights ought to be located with some care as there is no doubt whatsoever that when placed too close to plants with more tender leaves they will cause scorching of the foliage.

If you are using your conservatory for evening entertaining some well-placed spotlights and candles can create a beautiful setting for the meal.

▲ *A Bromeliad tree drips into a pool below.* (W Davidson)

▶ *Dramatic underwater lighting in a pool.*

▶▶ *A stunning pool surrounded by flowers.* (W Davidson)

6General Care

Watering and Feeding

If exotic plants are to be grown in the conservatory then one should endeavour to create some sort of 'feeling', a feeling of moistness in the air when one steps through the doorway into the green jungle.

If the floor of the conservatory is tiled or slabbed there should be no difficulty in running a can of water over the floor two or three times each day during warmer spells of weather. This treatment will reduce the need for watering the soil in the pots or in the beds where plants are set. Keeping the atmosphere damp reduces transpiration, which in turn means that the plants do not have to draw so much replacement water up through their roots.

When watering plants in pots, getting the right balance is the most difficult problem – too wet and the roots will tend to rot, causing eventual loss of leaves, and too dry will cause dehydration and an eventual shrivelling of the foliage. Some plants require a greater amount of water than others and this aspect will be covered under the notes on specific plants. If clean rain or stream water is available it will be better for the plants than hard tap water, but the latter is preferable to dirty water from a slimy rain water butt.

Generally speaking, from the time they are acquired, all plants will have to be fed with some form of nutrient, be it liquid, solid, or whatever. However, during the winter months the majority of plants will require no feeding whatsoever (see the gallery of plants for specific details). In any event, one should follow the feeding directions given with the product that is being used, bearing in mind that it is not in any way beneficial to the plant to feed it with greater concentration or more frequent feeding than is recommended.

Where the conservatory is more of a dual purpose garden room that is carpeted and furnished with plants as attractive accessories, then it is impossible to contemplate wetting the floor however much the plants may be in need of the moisture that results. For the garden room, it is usually better to have all plants in containers of some kind, and the best type of these will either be the self-watering type, or the hydroculture kind, both of which make watering a very much simpler exercise.

Self-watering Plants, Hydroculture and Half-hydro

Both have water reservoirs in their base which, in the case of self-watering units, is made available to the plant by means of capillary action, whereas the hydroculture plants are growing entirely in water. For both of these, the levels of water in the base of the units are controlled by water level indicators, and both types of units will go for three to four weeks between each filling with water. The self-water unit is fed with conventional nutrients, while the hydro-culture unit needs a special fertiliser that will be available from the supplier of the specially grown plants that are required for hydroculture.

Another growing concept that provides excellent results, though little used, is that of half-hydro. With this method one employs a watertight container,

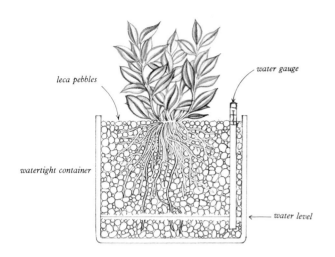

leca pebbles

water gauge

watertight container

water level

Hydroculture

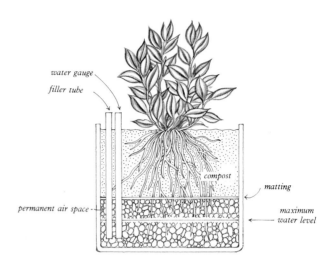

water gauge

filler tube

permanent air space

compost

matting

maximum
water level

Half-hydro

box or pit in the conservatory for the growing of plants. The bottom third of the container is filled with Hydroleca pebbles (resembling small hazel nuts and used in the building industry) on the surface of which is placed a complete covering of gauze matting that will allow plant roots to penetrate. The remaining two thirds of the container is then filled with potting compost into which the chosen plants are planted.

To control the amount of water that is required to grow plants successfully it is necessary to place a tube that extends from the bottom of the container to above the level of the soil – this is done as the infilling is undertaken. Within the tube there is a simple water level indicator – an indicator that can be made from a firm drinking straw that has one end glued to a table tennis ball. The ball floats on the water and the top end of the straw is visible at the top of the tube. The indicator should be so regulated to ensure that the maximum water level in the pebbles is about three inches between the matting and the soil.

The water level tube is some $1\frac{1}{2}$ in in diameter, and a second similar tube is also positioned alongside

the indicator tube through which water and special hydroculture nutrients can be supplied. Plants are placed in the upper soil in normal fashion and in time the roots find their way through the matting and into the nutrients at lower level in the water below and there is no question that when grown in this way the vast majority of plants grow exceedingly well. Roots that find their way into the lower level become much fatter and more succulent than soil roots which seems to have a marked advantage as far as the plants are concerned.

Potting on

One of the first duties on acquiring plants should be to inspect the root system, because in many instances the plants will require to be potted into a larger container immediately. But it should be remembered that only plants with a well matted root ball should be potted on, as it is detrimental to put plants into larger pots if they are not sufficiently established in their existing containers.

When potting on, choose a new pot that is only a little larger than the existing one, and use a properly prepared potting mixture and not a few shovels of soil that have been dug from the garden. Late spring–early summer is the best time for potting plants, but they can be done at other times if the growing conditions are good, but it is inadvisable to pot plants on during the winter months. After potting on, the soil should be watered thoroughly and left on the dry side until plants have resettled.

Many of the plants with large, glossy green leaves will have to be cleaned periodically, but one should never do this to excess. It is also harmful to use cleaning materials on leaves too often, and it can be fatal to apply chemicals and then to expose plants to bright sun or very cold conditions. Glossy leaved plants can be cleaned with a sponge that has been soaked in tepid water, and if dirt on leaves is difficult to budge, a very small amount of detergent in the water can work wonders. Never clean soft new leaves or leaves that are in any way hairy, such as those of the saintpaulia.

Improving Performance and Appearance

One of the greatest pleasures attached to having plants around one is that of physically caring for them, doing things that will improve their appearance, performance or whatever. It's a bit like having a boat, you don't just sail the boat, you have to do things to it to keep it up to scratch. With plants you don't just get pleasure from looking at and admiring them, you also get pleasure from attending to them by way of cleaning, potting and generally improving their appearance.

Cleaning the dust off the leaves has already been mentioned, but there is also a need for regular checks on re-staking, tying in, removal of dead leaves and such like. One of the interesting aspects of these varied exercises is that, like cleaning a car, you don't realise that there are so many scratches and defects until you get close up and begin to take that additional bit of notice. You can walk by a plant every

day and not notice that it is developing an infestation of greenfly or mealy bug, but when you get close up and begin to handle it you soon realise that all is not as it should be.

Simply handling plants and relocating them within the conservatory will give them a new and improved appearance. The spring or autumn thorough clean up is fine, but to be really effective you should physically handle your plants much more often than once or twice each year. It is not suggested that this exercise should become a fetish, whereby plants are forever on the move from one location to another with the result that they hardly know if they are coming or going, and deteriorate in the process.

If you have lots of plants in individual containers (and this can be one of the most interesting ways of growing plants in a conservatory) it is often not possible and seldom advisable to pot them on each year. In fact, if you were to pot a conservatory collection of plants annually they would soon outgrow the available space. Keeping plants in smaller pots will restrict their growth and make it possible for you to accommodate a larger and perhaps more interesting collection. There is little doubt that potting on improves the appearance of all healthy plants, but their general appearance can also be enhanced simply by adopting the old practice of top dressing. This simply means that with a pointed stick you loosen and remove the top two inches of soil from the top of the pot and replace it with fresh mixture. Not only will this simple duty get rid of algae forming around the top of the pot and all the dead bits and pieces that accumulate, it will also provide surface roots with additional nourishment.

Almost irrespective of the growing conditions and the ability of the owner of the conservatory it will be inevitable that in time older plants will shed lower leaves, often to the detriment of the plant. Some plants, such as the Cheese Plant, *Monstera deliciosa*, can become decidedly ungainly when reduced to a few top leaves and yards of bare stems with a few aerial roots protruding from them. Plants of such size will invariably be in pots of reasonable dimension which will allow for one, even two smaller plants to be planted in the soil alongside the main stem, or stems.

With reasonable care these young plants will become established so that their growth can be trained to the bare main stem of the plant to present a much more attractive appearance.

Many plants of the dracaena tribe will shed lower leaves as the plants increase in height, and with plants such as *D. deremensis* this will be inevitable as the plant grows naturally with a bare stem and tufts of growth at the top. However, there is no reason why one should not improve on nature and introduce one or two small climbing plants to the pot so that the bare stem can be concealed. Plants for this purpose could be chosen from *Rhoicissus rhomboidea* (Grape Ivy), *Philodendron scandens* (Sweetheart Plant) or *Ficus pumila* (Creeping Fig). All of these will have to be tied in and trained to the stem of the central plant, and will also benefit from having their growing tips removed occasionally to encourage a fuller appearance.

With two plants growing in the same container you will frequently find that growth is generally very much more vigorous, probably because moisture is absorbed more rapidly and roots do not lie too wet for too long.

Care in Your Absence

Although the general business of watering and such like is all part of the pleasure and interest attached to growing plants in the conservatory it can present difficulties when one is absent for one reason or another. If neighbours or acquaintances are delegated to care for plants during vacations, for example, it is very necessary to give explicit instructions concerning requirements, it being sound sense to write these directions down so that there is no confusion in the mind of the custodian during absences. The possibility is that the person left in charge is inexperienced so it is as well that they should have some form of guidance.

If you have fallen out with the neighbour, or the acquaintances have (perhaps wisely!) arranged to be absent at the same time as yourself then other methods have to be employed. It is worth investigating one or more of the drip watering systems that are available. These are little bother to install, and can be arranged so that each large pot has its own supply from one or two water drip valves, or smaller plants can be grouped together on a section of capillary matting so that a drip of water can be made available to the matting to keep it moist. If the small plants are in thin-based plastic pots the matting and soil will come into immediate contact so that the capillary action can induce a flow of water from the matting into the soil. The plants in small pots should be watered before they are placed on the matting.

Rather than fix up these capillary or tube watering devices the evening prior to departing on vacation one should run trials over a period of some weeks beforehand to ascertain just how much water is coming through and that plants are not likely to become excessively wet or too dry, depending on how well the apparatus performs.

Although the conservatory provides good growing conditions, care and attention are needed to ensure spectacular displays such as this one (plumbago and oleander). (Smiths)

7 Using the Greenhouse as a Feeder Unit

To manage a conservatory filled with a varied collection of exotic plants that are there for their flowers and/or their foliage the owner should also be conversant with the care of plants in greenhouse conditions (not that the two are all that different). The greenhouse should be a feeder unit that will maintain a regular supply of fresh plants for the conservatory, particularly flowering pot plants that are brought on to the point at which flowers are just showing colour before plants are transferred to the conservatory. Many of these plants will be annuals, such as schizanthus, which are discarded following flowering.

The Greenhouse as Hospital?

The greenhouse feeder unit is often looked upon as a hospital area for reviving ailing plants, but this is quite the wrong view to take. If the greenhouse is to be looked upon as a hospital or convalescent home for dead and dying plants from the conservatory then there is little chance that it will perform its proper function. The greenhouse will become ever more depressing with the result that you lose interest and all the plants fall into decline. When one has dead and dying plants it is very much better to make a firm decision to dispose of them. However, should the plant be a prized possession one should check to see what can be salvaged in the way of propagating material. Surprisingly, one will often find the odd bits of healthy growth on ailing plants, and these can be taken to the greenhouse and treated for pests before inserting them in the propagating case.

Nevertheless, the temptation to introduce pest-ridden cuttings that are weak and feeble should be avoided – these seldom make good quality plants, and pests can soon get out of hand in the warm conditions in greenhouses.

The Greenhouse as Nursery

Commercial pot plant production units are generally referred to as nurseries – places where plants are carefully nursed along from one stage to the next until such time as they have reached perfection and become ready for sale. The small greenhouse that is part of the conservatory unit should be looked upon in exactly the same way – one should start plants off from seed, cuttings or whatever and nurse them along until they are in condition considered suitable for the conservatory show place. The greenhouse ought to be heated so that plants may be overwintered successfully, and it ought to be benched all the way around two sides and one end so that the maximum number of plants can be accommodated.

Fitting out the Greenhouse

The materials from which they are made and the designs of greenhouses are even more varied than those of the conservatory, and a visit to one or two Garden Centres will indicate what one can expect in the way of value and service. The feeder greenhouses need not be too large but, like the conservatory, one will usually find that whatever size is chosen it will, in a few months' time, prove to be much too small for one's requirements. A sensible suggestion is to opt for a greenhouse that one can extend by fitting in extra sections as and when required.

Fitting out the greenhouse is not normally difficult as it is a purely functional building into which one should be able to put the maximum number of plants, provided they are not suffering as a result of overcrowding. Benching on two sides and at one end is the practical way of going about it or, if one intends to accommodate larger plants, it may be desirable to omit the end section of staging so that plants may be grown from floor level to whatever height the greenhouse may be.

If potted plants are to be grown in the greenhouse with the aim of keeping the conservatory well stocked, then it will be just as essential to retain a moist, growing feeling of humidity. As a means towards this end the raised staging should be covered with a moisture-retaining material of some kind. Three eighth size gravel from the local builder's yard will be an economical and simple way of doing this. About a 5 cm/2 in layer of these small stones will be necessary and, even when pots that are placed on the gravel are not watered, it will be essential to keep the gravel moist.

Sand can be used as an alternative, but there is a marked tendency for plants to root through into the sand, with the result that plants are damaged when it comes to time for breaking the roots off, either to relocate the plant or to pot it on.

If clean and efficient appearance is a requirement when covering the staging, you can use capillary matting as a base on which to place plant pots. Matting of this kind is now readily available and you should choose a material that is fairly thick and likely to last longer, besides retaining a great deal more moisture. The matting is laid smooth side down, and it will be an advantage if the matting can be taken outside periodically so that it can be thoroughly cleaned with a firm bristle brush. The matting must be kept moist. It will be found that plastic pots are much more suitable for use in connection with this material, as opposed to traditional clay pots.

Much controversy exists concerning the merits of plastic as opposed to clay containers for growing plants, but there is little doubt that clay pots have been on their way out for some considerable time. Clay pots have certain merits, and are ideal for plants such as sansevierias and yuccas which tend to become top heavy if they are growing in pots that are too light to provide sufficient anchorage. In any event, clay pots are the least suitable for growing plants that are to be placed on capillary matting, as the thick base prevents the soil in the pot coming into direct contact with the wet matting. Such being the case, the plant derives little benefit, whereas the plastic pot with its thin base ensures that the soil and matting come into immediate contact so that water may be drawn into the soil by capillary action.

A supply of electricity is important for the greenhouse enthusiast who wishes to work on after dark, and you must also have a supply to heat the propagating case that will almost surely become part of the greenhouse scene. Electricity will be needed for operating automatic ventilation and, possibly, for the warming cables that one may wish to place under the pots in which plants are growing.

Considerations for heating the greenhouse in which plants are to be reared are the same as those relating to the conservatory, with running costs and convenience being prime considerations. Sadly, one only learns about many of these aspects through experience, but it can be costly if the wrong choice is made at the outset. It is, therefore, important to go into all the pros and cons, and perhaps to take the step of joining your local Gardening Club which will normally abound with enthusiasts who will only be too pleased to put you in touch with greenhouse or conservatory owners who will be able to pass on all sorts of information about greenhouse and conservatory equipment – information that will be more relevant than simply taking everything that is contained in the brochures that may be available on the subject.

▲ *Even with a small conservatory such as this long, thin one you can ensure year round colour by bringing in new plants from the feeder greenhouse. The begonias in this picture are replaced with azaleas on page 50 bottom, in a view of the same conservatory.* (A W Jacobs)

◀*The greenhouse as feeder unit provides a constant supply of colourful plants for the conservatory.*

Plant Propagation in the Greenhouse

Plants may be propagated in a variety of different ways and almost all of them will offer some fascination for the interested plantsman.

Propagating from Seed

From a few packets of seed at very little cost one could quite easily provide sufficient plants to well fill the new conservatory, and this could well be the best initial move rather than to go in for established and expensive plants. The packets of seed will provide plants with a wealth of colour and as time goes on one can gradually extend the interests to more exotic and more permanent plants such as bougainvillea, stephanotis and the like.

Also, you will find, on looking along the shelves at the seeds that are on offer, that the seedsman has become more adventurous and there is now a fascinating range of subjects from which one can make a selection. The seed packet will give all the information that one is likely to need for sowing and general conditions required in order to get optimum results. However, it is wise not to go in for seed that will produce plants that are too vigorous in their growth, as they may be difficult to accommodate in the conservatory that will inevitably and rapidly become filled with plants. The interest in plants quickly grows and lots of them will be acquired from people with similar interests who have a surplus. It makes good sense to become a member of your local horticultural club where ideas and plants can be freely exchanged – you may in time even feel like exhibiting some of the treasures from the conservatory collection!

One of the most colourful and easiest of plants for the beginner to propagate is the Poor Man's Orchid, or schizanthus which can be sown at various times of the year, but is probably best done in August so that plants are available for a spring show of colour. Select one of the more compact varieties and sow them as recommended on the packet, then grow them on in good soil moving them to slightly larger pots as soon as roots are well established. If kept nourished and grown in good light, plants should be in pots of (15–18 cm) 6–7 in diameter by the spring of the following year to provide an amazingly bright display of colour.

In September one can sow seed of cyclamen (there are numerous fine strains to choose from) and these should be started in temperatures of around 21°C/70°F in order to obtain rapid germination. These are generally put into seed trays and are spaced about 3 cm/1½ in apart at the time of sowing. Once two firm leaves have appeared they are potted singly in small pots filled with a well-drained mixture of soil. Although they need high temperature during the germination period, it is essential that from then on cyclamen plants are grown in cool and airy conditions. For this reason it is usually best to use them as temporary decorative plants in the conservatory, returning them to the cooler conditions of the greenhouse when they have lost their sparkle.

Opposite to the cyclamen in temperature requirements are the smithianthas which need temperature of around 21°C/70°F when seed is sown in March/April, and thereafter reasonably warm conditions in order to produce their bright coloured flowers in late summer. The foliage is heart-shaped and velvety in texture which adds interest to the plant. Once established they develop tubers that can be retained from year to year if plants are given a dry and warm winter rest.

With brilliantly coloured trumpet flowers on short stalks the gloxinias are much easier to manage and can be grown from seed sown early in the year. Like the smithiantha, they will also develop tubers that can be retained for flowering in subsequent years if dried off and kept warm over winter.

Raising new plants from seed does not entail the purchase of costly equipment provided one has the basic requirement of a greenhouse to begin with. However, when the interest in propagation develops and one is attempting to make new plants from the various kinds of cuttings that may have been taken, then it is advisable to improve facilities in order that the success rate be improved. One of the most important attributes will be a heated propagating case in which cuttings will not only respond to the warm atmosphere that prevails in the propagator, but they will also be warm at their 'feet'. And when the 'feet' of cuttings, the base of the stem, are warm the chance of increasing the rooting percentage is considerably enhanced.

For the serious-minded propagator one of the best pieces of equipment will be a small mist unit which can be set to mist leaves with a fine spray of moisture automatically, or can be set to function as and when leaves dry out on their surface. There are some cuttings, the poinsettia in particular, for which a mist unit is an essential item if the rooting percentage is to be reasonable.

In other respects one should provide hygienic conditions in the way of clean containers for cuttings, fresh peat in which to insert them and, for some subjects, rooting hormone powder or liquid with which to treat cuttings prior to insertion.

Propagation from Cuttings

When taking cuttings from the parent plant the golden rule is to ensure that the material is sound and clean, and this will often entail the sacrifice of parts of the plant that one may feel can be ill spared. But for best results only the best propagating material will do.

Of the more common potted plants the Busy Lizzie, impatiens, is one of the easiest to propagate from cuttings. Of these the comparatively recent introduction of New Guinea hybrids shows a marked improvement over previous kinds. Many of these newer plants have attractively variegated foliage and develop into substantial plants if well watered and fed, and potted on as required. Many of the impatiens are not worth taking cuttings from as they are very easily raised from seed. Impatiens will root in water by covering a jar of water with kitchen foil, then making a hole in the foil for the stem of the cutting to be pushed through so that it can be suspended with the stem in the water. When taken from the water for potting in soil, the roots that have formed can be easily damaged and it is really as well to start cuttings in a peaty compost at the outset. Cuttings of this plant can be taken at almost any time of the year but it is advisable to remove any flowers before cuttings are inserted. In fact, flowers of all cuttings should be removed as dead flowers will tend to rot and cause unnecessary problems.

Saintpaulias can also be rooted in either water or peaty soil but, like the impatiens, will also be inclined to suffer a set back when potted from water to soil. The saintpaulia, African Violet, can be propagated from seed without too much difficulty, but it will be impossible to know the colour of plants raised in this way. To ensure that one is getting the identical plant repeated, it is essential to propagate new plants from leaf cuttings. To do this one should select the freshest and sturdiest leaves on the plant and reduce the leaf stalk to about 5 cm/2 in in length. Cuttings are then dipped in rooting powder, but if dry the stem can first be briefly dipped in water so that the rooting powder adheres in greater quantity to the leaf stalk.

Boxes or pots filled with peat will suit them fine, but it is important not to have leaves overlapping one another as this will result in new growth coming up in the dark, which can be harmful. If cuttings are going into pots, they should be placed around the edge of the pot with the leaves facing inwards. About half the length of the leaf stalk is buried in the peat, and it is best to make a hole of this depth with a pencil and carefully to place the cutting in the hole before firming the peat around it.

The secret of growing plants with a flat appearance and flowers standing cleanly away from them lies in the preparation of the cutting once it has produced a cluster of new leaves. When large enough to handle without damaging, the cutting is watered and taken from the soil and the cluster of plants at the base of the stem is carefully teased apart to reveal anything from five to ten minute plants. With great care these are then potted into individual tiny pots. The eventual result is that, as the plants have only one stem, all the new leaves that develop radiate from the central point to provide a neat, rounded appearance.

If one can avoid the temptation to water these plants to excess, it will be found that they will not only root better, they will also grow better.

The saintpaulia will root more readily in temperature of around 21°C/70°F, as will the poinsettia which develops its colourful bracts during the month of December. Following the natural shedding of bracts in March/April poinsettias should be rested and started into growth again by applying water to the soil when new growth is evident along the stem. At this time it is advisable to prune growth back to about 10 cm/4 in from the main stem and, if one desires to take cuttings, the new growth on the old stem should be allowed to make firm cuttings about 10 cm/4 in long before they are removed, leaving a small stump attached to the main stem of the plant. The cutting with its rich green leaves is then placed in a small pot filled with clean potting compost. Better results will ensue if small batches of cuttings can be done together, rather than solitary ones, and this applies to most plants.

Cuttings of poinsettia will generally flag alarmingly following insertion in the peat and it is at this time that continual misting of the foliage is essential. The ends of cuttings will callus over after some ten days and they will have their first roots in about three weeks.

Potted plants with smaller leaves are usually more successful if more than one cutting is placed in the pot when propagating. Plants that immediately spring to mind in this connection are the many fine tradescantias, the ivies and the Creeping Fig, *Ficus pumila*. All of these should have at least five cuttings in a 8 cm/3½ in pot to provide plants of full appearance. Also, with cuttings of this kind it is better to use a proper pot to insert them in, as young plants can be left to grow on in the same containers.

Propagating from Plantlets

Some subjects actually develop young plants that are perfectly formed while still attached to the parent. Most common of these are *Saxifraga sarmentosa* (Mother-of-Thousands), *Tolmiea menzies* (Piggyback

Plant, *Episcia dianthiflora* (Snowflake Plant) and *Ceropegia woodii* (Hearts Entangled). All of these produce small replicas of the parent in some way or another, and to propagate them it is simply a question of snipping them from the parent and potting them individually in small pots of clean peat or potting soil. These are perhaps the most encouraging of all plants for the beginners' initial steps into the mysteries of propagation.

The bromeliad family provides a wealth of fascinating plants, both for shape and for colourful flowering bracts. Leaves are produced in the form of a rosette, some large and some small, from the centre of which will emerge the bract. One drawback is that when the flower dies, so does the bract from which it emerged shortly after. To compensate for this, however, one will find that as the parent rosette deteriorates it will produce a small collection of identical bracts from the base of its stem. These can be left attached to flower as a cluster or they can be cut from the parent stump with a sharp knife and potted individually in peaty compost (the latter gives better results). In many instances roots will have already formed so there is no difficulty in getting plants under way again, but it does take several years for these new plants to produce flowers in their own right.

A less usual plant that produces young plants at the base of its stem is the pandanus, which can develop to majestic size in agreeable conditions. Plants of the pandanus can be increased by pulling these smaller plants away from the stem of the parent and potting them individually. As this is the only practical method of propagation it is inevitable that pandanus are destined to be ever in short supply.

Propagation by Air-Layering

There are many different types of ficus (Rubber Plant being one common name) and most of these are

▶ *The spring display of plants in this conservatory is achieved by using the greenhouse as a feeder unit. (R Aggiss)*

reasonably easy to propagate if the task is undertaken in November/December when there is less sap present in the stems of plants. Straightforward cutting up of stems and inserting leaves is one way to increase rubber plants, but the air-layering method for *F. robusta* can be that little bit more intriguing. (Air-layering is also one way of reducing the height of Rubber Plants that have outgrown their headroom.) To perform this propagating exercise one should remove a leaf about 30 cm/12 in down from the top of the plant, and then make an upward cut through the joint where this leaf was attached to the plant with a sharp knife. It is wise at this stage to have another pair of hands holding the plant to prevent it snapping at the point where the cut is made. It would be wise also to take the further precaution of placing a stout cane along the stem and tying it in position in the form of a splint. The cut stem is then held open by placing a piece of matchstick in the gap. Place a handful of wet sphagnum moss on either side of the cut. With a little dexterity a piece of polythene can be placed over the moss and tied firmly in position. In about eight weeks, with luck, one should see roots appearing inside the polythene. When the polythene is well filled with roots the stem can be cut below the polythene which is removed prior to potting the plant in a 12.5 cm/5 in pot filled with peaty compost. The stump of the tree that remains will develop growth from its topmost leaf axils and will generally provide a neater and more attractive plant.

8 Plant Problems

The conservatory that is maintained at agreeable temperature throughout the year will inevitably become a home for an assortment of pests and diseases. Pests may make their entry through an open door or window, but a surprising number will also appear on host plants that have been acquired in some way or another. Therefore, almost the first precaution is to ensure that plants that are introduced to one's collection are clear and free from problems (see Buying Plants on page 27).

Perhaps the most common source of infection lies in the plant that has been donated by an acquaintance who has learned that you have a brand new conservatory and feels that you must be in need of some plants to stock the place. Very often the gift is a plant that has outgrown its existing home and has a wealth of foliage and twining stems among which all manner of pests are likely to be found. Consequently one must treat all such gifts as suspect, even if it means offending the well-meaning donor.

It will also be found that the quality of your plants within the conservatory will have a bearing on the pest and disease problem. The healthier and more vigorous the plants then the more able they will be to withstand pest attack – the weaker the plant the more prone it invariably seems to be when pests are around. Maintaining proper control over the growing atmosphere within the conservatory will help considerably in fending off pest attack.

Conservatories that become very hot, or ventilators that are opened too wide when it is not necessary will result in a very dry atmosphere that will have a debilitating effect on plants. Pests, red spider mites in particular, will have a field day on plants that are grown in hot and dry conditions. Of all the likely pests the red spider mite is the greatest problem and one of the most destructive. This is a pest that has special preferences for particular plants, but it is quite capable of attacking almost any plant if there is nothing else to feed upon.

In conditions that tend to be very wet, there is a greater tendency for plants to develop fungal problems such as mildew and botrytis. To raise the internal humidity to counteract red spider it is not necessary to be forever pouring water into the surrounding plant pots. It is very much better to maintain a moist atmosphere by regular misting or by applying water to the floor. The latter is one good reason why it is advisable wherever possible to have a floor in the conservatory that will not be damaged by generally wet conditions.

It is extremely important to ensure when purchasing, certainly prior to application, that the chosen insecticide is suitable for the plants that are to be treated. If there should be plants in one's collection that may be harmed through the use of a particular spray, smoke bomb, or whatever, then one should remove these plants so that the others may be dealt with. Plants isolated in this way can be individually treated with a pesticide that is not likely to cause any damage.

The insecticide may be the most marvellous ever created with the most glowing accounts of experiments on particular plants, but it will be as much good as nothing if the material is not properly applied. If smoke type insecticides are to be used, seal the conservatory completely so that the insecticide will have the maximum effect.

If it should be a spray on insecticide, then be sure to use a sprayer that will ensure a good coverage that will thoroughly saturate the upper and lower surfaces of all foliage. If there are a lot of plants in need of attention then it is a good investment to purchase a sprayer of reasonable size that will ensure maximum coverage.

Some plants have so many small leaves and stems that it is almost impossible to make contact with every part of the plant simply by mixing a solution and spraying it onto the foliage. Ivies, or hederas, are perhaps the perfect plants to consider in this connection, as they have small congested leaves that can easily become infested with red spider mites. In this case, rather than spray the plant it is better to make up the solution as advised, in a bucket, and to perform the treating of the plant out of doors on a still day. The treatment amounts to placing a piece of polythene over the top of the pot to prevent the soil tipping out and then inverting the plant and immersing foliage in the solution. Hold the plant submerged until all the foliage has been well and truly saturated, then remove and stand the plant in a sheltered spot out of direct sunlight.

Needless to say, with all these operations one should wear rubber gloves, and take any other precautions that the insecticide manufacturer specifies on the bottle or package. All insecticides should be locked away in a cupboard that is well out of the reach of inquisitive young hands. Also, all utensils used when dealing with insecticides ought to be thoroughly cleaned before they are put away.

When new plants are introduced to one's collection of pest free plants it is wise to take the small precaution of treating the plant with a general insecticide just to be on the safe side. One of the simplest methods of doing this with smaller plants is to place the plant in a large polythene bag that is free of holes and then to put a few puffs of insecticide into the bag before sealing the top. The insecticide will have maximum effect and any obnoxious odours that may be given off by the particular insecticide will

Pests and problems

74

aphids

red spider

white fly

mealy bug

thrips

botrytis

mildew

be sealed within the bag, so causing no unpleasantness.

One application of a particular insecticide will be a futile exercise as far as many pests are concerned – white fly, for example require at least four applications at four day intervals to be reasonably sure that pests have been eradicated. Again, one should check manufacturers' directions for frequency of application with regard to particular pests.

Aphids

These are among the most persistent of pests and can be found on a wide range of plants, but usually on the tips of new growth. The term aphid covers a wide range of pests and chief among them are greenfly and blackfly. Both can multiply at a fearsome rate if not kept under control. Most prevalent in summer, these pests lay eggs that remain on plants throughout the winter to hatch out the following spring. There are numerous insecticides available for their control, and in a sealed off area it will be found that smoke bombs are effective, as well as being clean and easy to use.

These pests often cause more damage than one realises on seeing them cluster around soft new leaves. Being sucking insects they probe into the soft leaf with the result that when the leaf matures it will either be discoloured or have pit marks. A very ordinary houseplant that is affected in this way is the chlorophytum, and not everyone realises that discoloured leaves are the result of aphid when plants were quite small.

Red Spider Mite

Although not so easily detected as the aphids these are also pests that can multiply at a rate of knots if their presence goes undetected for any length of time. As mentioned earlier, they flourish in conditions that are hot and dry, and have distinct preferences for certain plants. The trained eye of the professional can usually see the signs of red spider being present on plants even before he has inspected the plants to ascertain that they are in fact there. The most common indication with green foliage plants is to note a hardening of the growth, and a yellowish discolouration of leaves that had hitherto been green.

They will also pay attention to tips of new growth and it is not unusual to see them moving rapidly to and fro on the fruits of the miniature Calamondin orange, Citrus mitis. For the untrained person, the best way of ascertaining that red spider is present is to get a magnifying glass (preferably a map reading one with a small light fitted) and carefully to inspect the undersides of the leaves in particular. Once you know what you are looking for, you can hold the infested leaf very still in order to see the mites going about their destructive business. Red spider is something of a misnomer as it is only the older members of the tribe that will be dullish red, while the vast majority will be flesh coloured.

Controlling these pests can be a serious problem and it is really very necessary to detect them at an early stage before they have got a firm grip on your plants. In fact, where leaves have turned yellow all over and the webs of these pests can be clearly seen on the undersides of leaves and in the area between the leaf and where it is attached to the petiole, there is usually little chance of saving the plant. It would be better to destroy it.

One should endeavour to maintain a moist atmosphere wherever possible and treat the plant under attack as soon as noticed with one of the many insecticides that are available. The regular use of systemic insecticides as a precaution is one of the most practical ways of keeping plants free of these pests. With systemic insecticides the poison is in the system of the plant, so eliminating sucking insecticides when they probe into the leaf sap.

There are numerous conservatory-style plants that the red spider mites have a penchant for – from the humble to the more exotic and delicate. Perhaps the lowest of the low is *Thunbergia alata* (Black-eyed Susan) which can prove to be host for literally thousands of these pests. Among the more exotic are the calatheas and the crotons, with *Acalypha hispida* seeming to be especially desirable to red spiders. The colourful croton, among the most exotic of purely foliage plants, will often have colouring that is similar to that of these pests, which makes detection all the more difficult. Of the more common flowering plants the hibiscus will often have more than its fair share of red spider mites.

Scale

These are pests that are only seen on plants that are growing in warm conditions, and are easily detected and not too difficult to eradicate if one is thorough when cleaning plants or applying insecticides.

Scale insects will attack all manner of plants and of these the pests are probably more easily seen on the Birds-nest Fern, *Asplenium nidus avis*. Scales will be seen on the upper and lower surfaces of leaves around the midrib. When detected, these pests can be wiped off the leaf by using a sponge that has been soaked in Malathion insecticide, not forgetting to wear rubber gloves. This treatment is probably the most effective for all the plants that have larger leaves. The other common indoor plant that will play host to scale insects is *Ficus benjamina*, the Weeping Fig.

Older scales are brown in colour and resemble tiny limpets, while the young members of the family are softer and flesh coloured. An indication of their presence is sooty mould forming on leaves below where scales are present.

White Fly

These are very persistent and can become a major problem if not given immediate attention when detected – frequent treatments being necessary with recommended insecticide if plants are to be completely cleared of their presence. Pay particular attention to the undersides of leaves and repeat the application of the chemical as often as the manufacturer suggests.

Prevention is better than cure and it is of the utmost importance when acquiring plants to inspect the undersides of foliage to ensure that these little white demons are not already in residence.

Mealy Bug

Like scale insects these are easily seen. The bugs themselves are powdery white in colour and they enclose their young in a waxy, cotton-wool-like shroud that protects them from almost everything in the way of insecticides. When treating plants that are infested it is essential to make very direct contact with the pests. If only a few plants are involved, then the bugs can be killed by dabbing them with methylated spirit which can be applied with an old toothbrush or cotton wool buds. Older plants that make a lot of growth in the upper reaches of the conservatory, especially stephanotis, are capable of harbouring large numbers of these unpleasant pests.

Thrips

Not such a difficult problem, but these can cause streaks of discolouration on the flowers of numerous plants that one may chance to grow in the heated conservatory. There are numerous insecticides available for their control.

Mildew

Of the fungal problem that might cause damage to one's plants, mildew is the most common. There are numerous plants that may be affected and chief among them are the many begonias, both foliage and flowering kinds, that one may have on display. White, irregular spotting on the surface of leaves is their trade mark, and is usually more in evidence when plants are growing in conditions that are stuffy and airless. Leaves that are very badly discoloured as a result of mildew should be removed and burned, and other leaves treated with appropriate fungicide.

Botrytis

Similarly, this problem is much aggravated by damp and close conditions, and is seen as a wet rot around congested leaves and leaf stalks. Cyclamen growing in poor light and airless conditions are very prone to botrytis which is mainly seen where leaves and flowers are attached to the corm in the centre. Affected plants should be thoroughly cleaned over before being treated with fungicide. It will also be important to improve the general growing conditions.

Index